Environment, Development and Military Activity

Towards Alternative Security Doctrines

JOHAN GALTUNG

Environment, Development and Military Activity

Towards Alternative Security Doctrines

UNIVERSITETSFORLAGET
Oslo – Bergen – Trondheim

© Universitetsforlaget 1982
ISBN 82-00-06360-7

Distribution offices:

NORWAY

Universitetsforlaget
Postboks 2977 – Tøyen
Oslo 6, Norway

UNITED KINGDOM
Global Book Resources Ltd.
109 Great Russell Street
London WC 1B 3NA

UNITED STATES and CANADA
Columbia University Press
136 South Broadway
Irvington-on-Hudson
New York 10533

Production arranged by
I · S UNDERVISNINGSLITTERATUR, Hans B. Butenschøn & Co
N-1914 Ytre Enebakk
Cover Photo: A-foto, Oslo
Printed in Norway 1982 by
Rogaland Industritrykk, Stavanger

Contents

5. TOWARDS RECOMMENDATIONS

Preface

There are those who say that there is little or no relation between the degradation of the environment and security matters. This book shows how false and dangerous that kind of thinking is. For a number of reasons.

First, science and technology – which ought to bring about increased well-being for all of humankind – have now brought us close to the absolute weapon, the Omnicidal Weapon that can destroy everything. The weapons of mass destruction do not only kill human beings. They destroy their settlements and the social fabric. They kill higher and lower animals, forests and green plants in general. They threaten the whole biosphere and the basis for life itself. They also destroy the rest of the environment, contaminate the atmosphere and the hydrosphere, pushing the lithosphere closer to processes of desertification. Ultimately they even tamper with outer space. No doubt the greatest threat to the environment are the weapons of mass destruction, particularly the nuclear arsenal. There can be no more urgent task in the struggle against environmental degradation than the fight against nuclear warfare.

Second, just as wars will lead to further degradation of the environment, an environment less able to sustain human societies as we know them today may easily lead to even more wars, in a struggle for ever scarcer resources, such as uncontaminated soil and water. This is a vicious circle we cannot afford to be dragged into.

But, it may be objected, we know much of this by now. What is needed is not so much to be convinced of the horrible consequences of nuclear war as to find some way out of the trap we have fallen into. And this is the third point: much of the book is devoted to the search for an alternative security doctrine based on less vulnerable societies and on defensive weapons that would cost much, much less than the current arsenal and put less pressure on scarce resources. This is done

7

following ecological principles, showing yet another linkage between environment and security: in ways of thinking.

Professor Galtung wrote this book when he was working as a special consultant for UNEP, assisting in our preparations for the Second Special Session on Disarmament of the General Assembly of the United Nations, New York, June–July 1982.

Ulf Svensson
Director, UNEP Regional Office for Europe

Author's preface

For a researcher who has been working for some years in the field of peace studies and on the goals, processes and indicators of development, to contemplate the ultimate effects of weapons of mass destruction on environment and development is to face the negation of all one hopes and struggles for. The abyss is open. And yet, merely to describe it and decry it seems insufficient, regardless of how well this is done. The challenge is to try to comprehend it in a way that also points to some way out of it or even around it. The present study is one such effort. There are others, fortunately.

I have benefited enormously from the brainstorming and consultations organized by the UNEP Regional Office for Europe, 21–23 November 1981 and 24–25 March 1982. I would like to express my deep gratitude to Ulf Svensson for organizing this, to everybody involved in the discussions and particularly to Dr R. A. Novikov and Dr A. H. Westing. The excellent work by Dr Westing is found all over in this field, through his publications for SIPRI and other places. But the responsibility for the presentation and the conclusions and recommendations is mine alone.

Bois Chatton, May 1982

Johan Galtung
Geneva International Peace Research Institute, Geneva
International Peace Research Institute, Oslo

1. The environment, development and military systems

1.1. The double problem

My concern here is with a double problem. First, there is the problem facing humankind today: for the first time in human history it has become possible not only for humankind to destroy so large a fraction of itself that the term *genocide* becomes applicable, but also to destroy the social fabric itself, both material and nonmaterial components, so that one can talk about *sociocide*. And in addition to this major parts of the environment, including the mechanisms sustaining it, can be destroyed so that one can talk about *ecocide*. And this is what there is to destroy:

$$\text{genocide} + \text{sociocide} + \text{ecocide} = \textit{omnicide}$$

The second problem is how to come to grips with all of this conceptually in such a way that not only are the implications of weapons of mass destruction clearly seen, but some possiblilities for averting such disasters also emerge clearly. For this a rich conceptual scheme is needed. Experiments with forms of exploration and forms of presentation are also needed. Fortunately, the literature in this field is now becoming rich and diverse.

It was mentioned above that this is a unique situation in human history. Of course, the plague in the middle of the 14th century in Europe (with its parallels in other parts of the world), the Black Death, was also a terrible disaster, according to some estimates killing 40% of the population. But the "nuclear death" from the most important of the weapons of mass destruction, the White Death[1] (from the light of a nuclear explosion), has a potentially much deeper impact. The Black Death touched only live matter; it did not destroy the social and environmental infrastructure except insofar as it had to be tended by human beings. And it did not touch the lower ranges of the biosphere, nor inorganic matter. It was like a cat's paw relative to the White Death. Weapons of mass destruction may destroy not only life, social order and the environment, but also the mechanisms that make possible regeneration/renewal of the quality and quantity we are used to and want, within a reasonable time frame.

How has this become possible? No doubt because of three essential differences between the periods of the Black Death and the White Death six centuries later: the introduction and growing complexity of science, making it possible to release nature's forces for good and for bad on a hitherto unknown scale;[2] the introduction and growing complexity of large-scale, world-encompassing organizations of a bureaucratic and/or corporate nature based upon state-formation and capital-formation with seemingly incompatible interests; and the growing complexity of the particular aspect of the state known as the military. The last decades have witnessed the growth of the military-bureaucratic-corporate-intelligentsia (MBCI) complexes to an unprecedented size. Of course the Black Death was also, to some extent, a society-inflicted curse: human beings travelled and with them parasites (hosted above all by rodents), carrying the lethal bacteria on ships, in caravans. Thus, people served indirectly as highly effective carriers of the "weapons" of their own destruction. The major difference, but indeed a perplexing one, is that this time the spread of destruction may be deliberate[3] if it should happen, and not only a capricious aspect of nature's doings with some human assistance. In short, we are in the rather peculiar situation where humankind not only develops the means of collective suicide but also sees to it that the result shall be to some extent irreversible, by cutting off the basis for sustaining life itself.

How does one deal with such an issue? We cannot get at its peculiar nature by studying only the relation between military activity and the environment, or military activity and society. The military activity we are dealing with here not only involves both of them, but also has a substantial impact on the relationship between environment and development. In order to understand the phenomenon more fully the whole environment-development-military systems triangle has to be explored, with implications running in all directions in the triad. This is particularly important because the seeds of military activity are also located somewhere in the environment/development interface, and not only inside the military system itself. To see this some simple conceptualizations of the three corners of this triangle will be presented in the following sections.

So the problem is on the one hand one of *survival,* on the other hand one of *comprehension* of the problem. To the latter there are many approaches, and they are contending approaches, none of them with a monopoly on validity. The present approach is more holistic than some others. This may open for some insights, but may also close for others more based on detailed insight in one or a few components of the systems only. Of course the choice of dimensions of analysis predetermines the possible conclusions or recommendations – and vice versa. This also applies to a more holistic approach: it will tilt the analysis towards holistic conclusions because so many interconnections, "linkages", can always be found within a sufficiently rich conceptual scheme. The result may easily be an unrealistic demand for a change of everything, or a fatalistic reconciliation with the change of nothing.

The present approach attempts a middle course. The conclusion is holistic and touches the whole environment-development-military systems triangle. It is in this triangle that a security doctrine can be described. But it is also within this triangle that *alternative security doctrines,* giving to the environmental, developmental and military systems their due, both in peace and war, can be proposed. It is not by chance that such thinking comes out of studies that also focus on the environment, not because the environment is in and by itself more or less holistic than the developmental and military systems, but because the science of environment, ecology, is so holistic. Environment thinking is inspiring, and for this reason, too, it seems appropriate to start in the environment corner of the triangle. And it is basic: respect for the environment is a *sine qua non* for us all.

1.2. Environment

The environment is a *set of components,* and in this set there is a *system of interaction.* It is customary and convenient to divide the environment into four systems: *atmosphere* (with tropo-, strato- and ionosphere), *hydrosphere, lithosphere* and *biosphere,* the first three being abiotic, the latter covering the biotic areas. To this one could add outer space or the *cosmosphere.* And one could also single out for spe-

13

cial attention within the biosphere humans and their settlements, or the *homosphere*.[4] The problem is how much subdivision should be made within the spheres. Obviously this is a problem of striking a compromise between such crude distinctions that the exploration becomes too general (the above division into spheres being an example of a very crude but still useful distinction) and such fine distinctions that the exploration gets lost in details.

After some trial and error the typology in Table 1 was adopted as sufficient for the purpose of this study. For each sphere there is first a short list of key components, then some aspects of the interaction systems. Thus, for the atmosphere the relevant system is also known as *climate;* for the biosphere it is known as *eco-systems*.[5] The whole typology is organized along Comteian-Darwinian lines, from the "lower" to the "higher" (as seen by humans). But this is also, by and large, an organization from the more to the less robust, from the less to the more vulnerable to insults of various kinds, including insults due to military activity.

The basic key to the functioning of the total global eco-system, from an anthropocentric point of view, would be:

Figure 1. *The six spheres and the feedback loops*

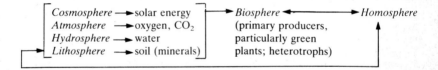

Everything relates to everything, but the arrows above indicate the crucial connections. From the cosmo-, atmo-, hydro- and litho-spheres come the key inputs to the primary production in the biosphere, of sugar, particularly by the green plants – chlorophyll being the basis, also found in some bacteria and other organisms capable of photosynthesis (phytoplanktons). The primary *producers* or *autotrophs* would also include sulphur bacteria and iron bacteria. Then comes the chain of *consumers* or *heterotrophs,* starting with the primary consumers that by definition are herbivores, and then the secondary consumers, the carnivores and omnivores up to four levels, in marine systems even one or two more levels. At the end of this food chain (or, better, food

Table 1. Environment: a typology of components and interaction

COSMOSPHERE
Components:
   bodies (celestial)
   space

Interaction:
   energy transfer (light, heat,
   ultra-violet rays, etc)

ATMOSPHERE
Components:
   oxygen
   nitrogen
   CO_2, H_2O
   ozone
   space

Interaction:
   temperature
   water (including precipitation)
   drought
   winds, hurricanes, typhoons
   lightning

HYDROSPHERE
Components:
   inland waters
   oceans, off-shore
   oceans, high seas

Interaction:
   waves, tsunamis, floods

LITHOSPHERE
Components:
   fossil fuels
   minerals
   soil
   area

Interaction:
   landslides, avalanches, soil erosion
   earthquakes
   volcanoes

BIOSPHERE
Components:
   micro-organisms
   plants
      lower (non-flowering)
      higher (flowering)
   animals
      lower (invertebrates)
         (molluscs, crustaceans, insects)
      higher (vertebrates)
         cold-blooded (reptiles,
            amphibia, fish)
         warm-blooded (birds, mammals)

Interaction:
   desert
   tundra
   grassland
   forest
      tropical
      temperate
         non-conifers
         conifers
   fires

HOMOSPHERE
Components:
   humans, human artefacts
   human settlements
      (in order of magnitude):
      single farms 10^1
      nomadic communities 10^2
      settled communities (villages) 10^3
      towns 10^4
      cities 10^5
      metropoles 10^6
      megalopoles 10^7

Interaction:
   micro-space (peer groups)
   meso-space (local level)
   macro-space (national, regional, global levels)

web) for energy/matter/nutrient exchange come the *reducers,* converting the organic compounds produced by the autotrophs to inorganic compounds in processes of mineralization and nitrification. The net result is eco-systems that tend to become highly diversified, and stable when equilibria have been attained, consistent with the abiotic context, which may be destructive, even disruptive, through nature's own interaction.

Humans are located at the higher trophic levels, capable of being primary consumers (herbivores, "vegetarians"), and secondary consumers (carnivores, meat-eaters). The focus in recent years has been on how humans degrade the eco-systems through air pollution, which may also impact on the solar energy reaching through the atmosphere, water pollution and soil pollution (pesticides and other wastes that are toxic and/or non-degradable). It would be important to know whether this degradation not only includes pollution of all inputs to primary production, and reduction in the number of primary producers, but also affects the production *process* itself, over and above this. In addition humans degrade eco-systems by simplifying them through agriculture (horticulture, forestry) and have to compensate for this with artificial fertilizers and pesticides. And on top of this comes the increasing number of human consumers and a tendency to consume at higher trophic levels; irrational since there is a substantial loss of energy from one trophic level to the next (in addition animals move and need energy for that). In short: *eco-crisis*[6].

In broad terms the homosphere depends on the biosphere and would disppear without it, humans themselves not being primary producers. The same applies to the other consumers, animals and some plants. The primary producers, in turn, depend on the inputs from the other four spheres. So, of course, do the consumers, consuming directly, not only via the food chains, solar energy, oxygen and water. In short, if one should remove any of the first spheres the primary producers would die out, and if they are removed the consumers – including the humans – would die out. The dependency chain is quite clear.

But this relation of dependency (in the *sine qua non* sense of necessary conditions) is not symmetric. If humans were removed the biosphere would continue and actually be better than before, since human agents of ecosystem degradation would have been removed, leaving the nonhuman sources of disruption alone: hurricanes, drought, lightning, floods, avalanches, earthquakes and volcanoes. It would have been interesting to be able to compare directly human-made and non-human-made environmental degradation in terms of order of magnitude, the latter sometimes being used as an excuse for the former. But regardless of what the conclusion would be, if for a moment we permit ourselves an anthropomorphic approach to (the rest of) nature: nature would not miss humans if we were to disappear but would on the contrary be relieved. And in the same vein one might add that the first four spheres do not depend on the biosphere either, but can do without it. Inside the biosphere the disappearance of birds and mammals in general (not only humans) would probably not matter much, since they are consumers only. But if plants are removed not only the biosphere dies, but the atmosphere loses oxygen (to nitrogen and CO_2), and the lithosphere suffers massive soil erosion. Consumers die since they are predators; and humans, it seems, are the greatest predators of all. That humans depend on the rest and the rest not on us should, perhaps, have inspired some modesty and care – but the opposite seems to be the case.

The key concern with ecosystems in this connection is the problem of *recovery* after some disturbance has been brought into the system. A distinction should be made between human-assisted and unassisted recovery, focussing to start with on the latter, with no human inputs. This is the natural healing power of the system; the system's ability to renew, regenerate itself. No doubt there is a built-in conservatism in this concept: it presupposes that the system as it was is worth regenerating. But even though this may not be the case, it is the system to which we have, or had, to some extent adapted as our basis of sustenance. This basis can be improved through human inputs. But it can also deteriorate, as evidenced in the phenomenon of desertification. By and large alternative systems, if not brought into being with great care, could easily become inferior.[7] Nature is still in most regards wiser than human beings!

At the more shallow level[8] of analysis, an eco-system's ability to renew itself is expressed in terms of compensatory production of and by the system itself, and its ability to absorb and degrade pollutants. Humans can best assist by not depleting nonrenewable resources, consuming with care renewable resources, and/or recycling the nonrenewable ones. Further, they can assist by producing only waste that is degradable and not toxic and can enter the eco-cycle again – banning the practices of trying to disperse the pollutants in diluted form in atmosphere or hydrosphere, and/or hiding them in remote parts of geographical and social space. In short depletion and pollution control.

At the deeper level of analysis one would add more perspective to these considerations. Crucial in the theory of renewal/regeneration, or recovery, is the concept of *resilience,* the robustness of the ecosystem. This is essentially the stable equilibrium concept referred to above, the equilibrium being dynamic rather than static.

Basic stability is maintained, although several variables, even key variables, are changing all the time. Some of this change is an important factor contributing to the stability of the equilibrium, such as the light and temperature cycles; some is merely destructive. A dynamic, not static, system is generally better prepared to meet insults.

Stable equilibrium in ecosystems depends on the level of *maturity* of the system, and maturity can be seen in terms of two key variables: the *level of diversity* (simply the number of types of biota) and the *level of symbiosis* among all the components.[9] In human and social systems we seem to be particularly concerned with the type of symbiosis which is equitable,[10] often in pairs, constituting a kind of unity between the two components: friendship, love, and sexual union being important examples. In ecosystem analysis, however, this would be a very special case indeed. As mentioned above, the focus is on cycles rather than pairs, with abiota being processed into biota and then consumed (meaning killed) along food and energy conversion chains (with humans on the top in the sense of being preyed upon by nobody but themselves) – and biota then ultimately being degraded into abiota. For this symbiosis – predatory and brutal rather than equitable and cooperative – to operate in such a way that the *system* moves towards maturity, a certain composition and level of diversity is needed. If that diversity is seriously reduced, or the abiotic components disturbed or disrupted, some input has to be supplied artificially, e.g. in the form of pesticides and artificial fertilizers, with potentially adverse effects. Otherwise the system may die out. Permanent intervention is needed to maintain an artificial system.

Seen holistically, from this type of system rather than component level of analysis, the key to ecosystem stability is maintenance of species diversity above a critical minimum (which may be relatively low), and maintenance of the ecocycle. A first condition here is obviously that primary producers are not destroyed and that the abiotic components are not disturbed or disrupted; a second that consumption does

18

not get out of hand, and a third that reduction can take place. Depletion means decrease of species diversity, possibly even primary production capacity. Pollution means destruction of inputs for primary production, and also overloading of reduction capacity. Essentially it becomes a question of keeping the cycle going, which presupposes diversity and symbiosis among the components.

Maturity has its limits, however. It may also become so high that the system loses some of its dynamic character and becomes more static and vulnerable. It is probably safe to assume that the level of maturity is a variable with its optimum in the middle range rather than at either end. It is also at the middle range that the biomass productivity (of micro-biota, plants and animals) is highest.

In general terms recovery of grassland after major insults is a question of decades, for forests of centuries. Deserts and tundras are very robust, but when destroyed extremely slow recovery rates have been observed. For agriculture the human inputs would obviously be considerable so recovery can be quicker if inputs are available. However, the robustness of deserts and tundras does not help humans much as their productivity of biomass is so low. With some exceptions this is a general principle: the more directly dependent humans are on the component the more vulnerable it is, and the less direct the dependence, the more robust the component.

So-called primitive humans were doing the ecologically safest thing: living off the biomass they could gather towards the end of its life-cycle, before the biota are being turned into abiota by the reducers. Through agriculture biomass productivity has been increased considerably – with the potentially very adverse side-effects. One might ask: cannot humans do better than this? Would it not be possible to increase biomass productivity even further and at the same time help nature to build more stable ecosystems by increasing the level of maturity where it is threatened? Generally speaking, this would mean increasing diversity rather than simplifying even further, reaping biomass for human consumption off more, and not less complex eco-systems capable of both renewal and waste absorption. Maybe we still know far too little or go about it the wrong way. Some interesting openings seem to have been found recently in the concept of self-sustaining eco-systems with high productivity, a nature improved upon by humans.[11] Unless new side-effects turn up. . .

1.3. Development

Development can also be seen in terms of components, human beings and their artefacts, with a system of interaction, a social system or society. This means that there are two types of, or aspects to development: *human development* and *social development.* That they are related goes without saying: human beings need a social setting for their development, at least a minimum setting; otherwise they will not even develop language. And society needs human beings to fill positions in the social structure, at least a minimum number if any sociotype is to survive.

Just as the environment can be divided into spheres with interaction not only within the spheres but also among them, development can be divided into sectors, aspects, dimensions (Table 2). But there is a crucial difference. We are used to looking at the environment as a natural system evolving according to a set of knowable and partly known laws, according to a code of its own that does not depend on human consciousness – and we tend not to endow nature with any consciousness. Development is regarded in a different way, more normatively, less descriptively. Human beings and societies, as parts of the biosphere (singled out above as the homosphere), may evolve according to a biological code, knowable and partly known. But it will also be steered by a civilizational code particular to the civilization of the society, knowable but usually unknown, as a set of unquestioned assumptions: *cosmology*. And it will be steered by a political program, not only knowable but highly explicit and known: *ideology.* Thus, there is a relatively universal factor in development linked to human biology, a civilizational factor and a political factor. If there were only the former, then development studies would be a part of environmental science. But civilizational (or cultural) diversity, and political differences, make the subject much more complicated. This complexity can only disappear in a world with only one dominant civilization, one cosmology, and only one dominant political ideology.[12]

One might try a formulation in one sentence: *The goal of development is adequate and sustainable satisfaction and further development of human needs – material and nonmaterial – and the process of development includes building institutions for production of basic needs, with priority for those most in need, in an equitable and self-reliant structure, consistent with ecological balance, culture and development of others.*

Table. 2. Development: a typology of human and social dimensions

HUMAN DEVELOPMENT
Sustainable satisfaction and development of human needs so as to facilitate, or at least not impede, the human development of others, with neither under- nor over-consumption of "satisfiers"

SOCIAL DEVELOPMENT
Human-made environment compatible with human development and so as to facilitate, or at least not impede, the social development of others.

(1) *Survival needs* (Negation: violence)
– for realization of potential biological life-span, unhampered by direct and structural violence; for reproduction

(2) *Wellbeing needs* (Negation: misery)
– for food, clothes/shelter, health care, schooling, "comfort", transportation/communication; for energy etc.

(3) *Identity needs* (Negation: alienation)
– for closeness to self and others; to society, culture and nature; for something to believe in; spiritual needs

(4) *Freedom needs* (Negation: repression)
– for the possibility of a choice in how to satisfy the other needs; for consciousness of choice

(5) *Production*
– in a broad sense (formal and informal; goods and services), with the priority of production to the satisfaction of basic human needs, then for further development

(6) *Distribution*
– so that priority is given to those most in need, building *social justice* and increasing *equality* among classes, racial and ethnic groups, sex and age groups, within and among countries

(7) *Institutions*
– building institutions for the implementation of these goals, avoiding excessive sectorialism and giantism

(8) *Structure*
– building equity at all levels with shared control over means of production – building, through participation, *self-reliance* at the local, national and regional levels – as much as possible with self-sufficiency in production for the most basic needs and equitable exchange for the rest

(9) *Culture*
– doing all this in a way compatible with those aspects of the endogenous culture that are compatible with the above

(10) *Nature*
– maintaining and building, on a sustainable basis, ecosystems with optimal level of maturity to prevent depletion and pollution

Thus, "development", which takes place at the expense of others, today or in the future, through inequity and/or dependency today, or environmental degradation, destroying the basis of sustenance for future generations, should not be referred to as "development" but as "exploitation". Such processes have to be counteracted with actions of solidarity with present and future generations (synchronic and diachronic solidarity); such actions themselves being part of development processes.

Of formulations such as this there are many in the international literature and fora. Their usefulness will always have to be tested, in practice and also in theory. One point should, however, be emphasized: the goal of development, and the process of development, is not only one of these points, but the total package. There is a totality, a *holisis* to development; an intuition only partly captured in such lists. At the same time this is intended as the type of definition that permits a wide array of possible implementations, a broad range rather than a point definition.

The centerpiece in the definition is human development, conceived of as the satisfaction of four classes of basic human needs. If these needs are not satisfied humans will disintegrate, satisfaction of basic human needs being a necessary condition for development, and their negation being a sufficient condition for disintegration.[13] The latter is clearly seen in the case of violence and misery. But it also holds for the nonmaterial needs for identity and freedom. A person has to have identity with something, self or others, society, culture (including religion and language), nature. There must be something to believe in. The alienated person is displaced, dis-integrated from the rest of humankind. And the repressed person is without *space*, without a chance of moving physically or mentally. These latter two, identity and freedom, are the being/becoming dimensions along which unlimited human growth is possible – towards higher levels of union or unity with self (self-realization), others (love), society (dedication), culture (deepening), nature (empathy) – and unity with something transpersonal, secular or sacred. The other two – survival and wellbeing – are having dimensions and here there are limits to growth set by the production that can be eked out of the ecosystems. Consequently, whether the civilizational code (and political ideology) focuses more on the being/becoming or the having dimensions is crucial to the style of development. Thus, the Western style is said to be more materialistic, and some Oriental styles, above all the pure Buddhist (particularly theravada), are in the nonmaterial direction.

The basic question, however, in development theory has been not so much focussed on the goals of development as on the process. Given a vague but relatively broad consensus that development has to do with satisfaction of basic needs the question is: which institutions can deliver the goods? Should there be more emphasis on market or on plan? on national or local levels? – These are key questions asked in the context of economic and political development. One possible answer, to give the bias of the present author, would be plan *and* market, national *and* local – with direct democracy at the local level, representative democracy at the national level and a federal structure coordinating the two. There are many answers to these questions, but solutions that place a lot of emphasis on plan *or* market seem to give to bureaucratic *or* corporate institutions so much power that popular participation becomes difficult. The same applies to too much emphasis on the national level, and also to too much emphasis on the local level "Small is beautiful", but "some big is necessary" or so it seems.

But even if there is no consensus in such matters there may still be considerable consensus as long as the formulations are not made too precise. Thus, there can be agreement about survival, wellbeing, identity and freedom even if there is very little agreement about the process needed to arrive at these goals. One reason for this disagreement may be that there is *some* empirical validity of all social doctrines (meaning a body of thought as to which processes lead to which goals), but the doctrines come as packages with "believe everything or nothing" written on them. For this reason no development doctrine is presented here, only the list of dimensions with some very broad indications of goals and processes – well knowing that the goals will always be in process, and the process will always tend to become a goal in its own right. The conceptual system should be open, flexible.

In conclusion some words about two key aspects of the definition: *solidarity* and sustainability or *security,* and on some of the dynamics between human and social development and between development and environment.

Human and social development are seen as incompatible with growth at the expense of other humans and other societies. Put more positively: a person humanly developed will also help to build human development in others; a society socially developed will also help to build social development in others. If two persons do this for each other it is called friendship, even love. If two societies do this for each other it is described in more prosaic terms: cooperation, integration, harmony; even peace (meaning positive peace as opposed to negative peace, the absence of violence). This is more than "interaction for mutual benefit". The two, or more for that matter, have to a certain extent become parts of each other, in each other's internal sector, and not in the "external sector" as an object for exploitation, to put it that way. With this addition the theory of development becomes less atomistic and egotistic, more systemic and solidarity-oriented.

The security aspect is where development starts bordering on military matters. It is a problem of protecting the system against change imposed upon it from within or without, through illegitimate force or by the threat of using force. The problem is how this protection can best be obtained, and this is the question of *security doctrine*. Security is also something to be produced by an institution with a certain structure, and distributed, with more or less respect for the ecological balance, culture and security of others, in a more or less egalitarian, just and equitable manner when it comes to the sharing of costs, risks and benefits. It is certainly one of the most controversial aspects of the whole development problématique, and it is to be deeply regretted that it is so rarely discussed in conjunction with other aspects of development and environment. We shall return to it in Chapters 4 and 5.

Development, then, is a question of identifying those processes whereby human development may strengthen social development and social development strengthen human development so that a virtuous circle is established. Two such processes can readily be identified from what has been said above, and we shall return to them later.

First, at the individual level the very concept of human development should induce high levels of solidarity with other human beings and other societies. The difficulty is clear: the concept becomes too abstract and vague. Solidarity is more likely to be in circles drawn closer to oneself, in which case a more modest notion enters, that of tolerance, particularly of that which is different. The reward should be in terms of reciprocity, whether formulated positively as "do unto others what you want others to do unto you" or negatively.

Secondly, at the social level one might conceive of social development so that it rewards cooperation and solidarity rather than competition and ruthlessness. A society systematically rewarding competition

24

will have to come to grips with the losers both intranationally and internationally; a society rewarding cooperation should, in principle, itself be rewarded by cooperation at both levels. And this has implications for the doctrine of security, as will be seen later. In practice, of course, all societies are a mixture of cooperation and competition.

Eco-development is the exploration – in practice and also in theory – of the interfaces between environment and development. The task of eco-development is to identify those processes that enhance the environment and at the same time strengthen development, not merely to explore the constraints the environment puts on development and the demands development makes on environment. Ideally one should find processes that lead to a virtuous circle whereby the two strengthen each other, as suggested above for human and social development.

Are there such processes? We are used to thinking only in terms of the opposite, of how development patterns make increasingly exhorbitant demands on the environment, with ecosystem instability and increasing deterioration as the consequence. But some positive linkages can be envisaged. Natural systems should be seen as potentialities, not only as constraints.

First, at the individual level one might link human development to a higher level of identification with nature, an empathy to the point where one feels part of nature (and nature part of oneself). In that case ecosystem deterioration would be felt, with compassion, as nature suffering, and one would be inclined to help. Such help would also be self-help; it would pay off in yielding a better basis of sustenance from a more productive ecosystem in return.

Second, at the local level one might link social growth or development to more local control of eco-cycles by organizing production-consumption cycles to that they are both transparent and controllable at the local level because people suffer the consequences (in depletion and pollution terms) of their own irrational behavior.[14] Eco-cycles spanning whole nations, regions or the whole world are neither comprehensible nor really controllable. Again this would be help for self-help, paying off in the form of a more productive and reliable ecosystem.

1.4 Military activity

Into this precarious balance between environment and development – the effort of societies now and in the past to steer a course between the outer limits set by a finite environment and the inner limits of satisfying basic needs for an expanding human population – we now introduce military activity.[15] As for environment and development, a distinction will be made between the military as a set of components and as a system of interaction, referring to the two parts as *military preparation* and *military action* (Table 3).[16] The term "action" has been preferred to "use" since there is also use of military components in connection with preparation, such as testing and maneuvers. And deployment is also use, as are threats of use and occupation, even if it is not exactly military action in the sense of destruction. Correspondingly, the term "arms race" has been avoided. The military institution involves so much more than just the hardware components referred to as "arms". And whether there is a race, in arms or in the whole military system in general, is an empirical hypothesis to be tested, not a taxonomic category for this purpose.[17] Under contemporary conditions "race" seems to describe the factual condition relatively well, but the term "military preparation" has been preferred, subsuming under it phenomena often referred to as the "arms race".

The list of components of military *preparation* is a social system. It has its culture, called "doctrine". As institution within the society in which it is embedded it has a structure, called "organization". It has a population called "humanpower". And it is concerned with the production of what essentially are means of destruction, enhancing the security of the system according to the doctrine. The production cycle is like any other production cycle, starting with research and development/testing, then production which (like any other production) uses production factors (natural resources, capital, labor, research, organization). After stockpiling comes the only peculiarity of the military system so far: it is prepared for action without real action (training/ maneuvers and deployment). Very much like other production cycles there is the element of secondary production in other countries, e.g. under license, and trade – both under the special heading of "proliferation". Thus, the terminology differs, which is useful. In spite of similarities, there are important differences between the development system and the corresponding components of the military subsystem: the difference between construction and destruction.

26

Table 3. Military activity: a typology of components and interaction

MILITARY PREPARATION

    Doctrine

    Organization
      structure
      capital

    Humanpower
      quality (mentality and
        education/training)
      quantity (numbers)

    Research
      humanpower
      research facilities

    Development/testing

    Production/stockpiling
      land, raw materials
      energy
      capital
      labor
      production facilities;
        organization
      storage facilities

    Training/maneuvers

    Deployment
      domestic
      abroad (bases; land/sea,
        outer space)

    Proliferation
      secondary production
      trade

MILITARY ACTION

    Piercing/impact

    Incendiary
      flames
      heatflux
      oxygen consumption

    High explosives
      blast
      high velocity fragments

    Chemical/toxic

    Biological

    Radiological

    Nuclear
      electromagnetic pulse
      blast
      thermal radiation
      ionizing radiation
      – initial (primary)
      – radioactive fallout (secondary)

    Geophysical
      biosphere (fires)
      atmosphere (climate, ionosphere,
        ozone, lightning)
      hydrosphere (tsunamis,
        ocean currents, river floods)
      lithosphere (earthquakes, vol-
        canoes, landslides, avalanches

In the list of components for military *action* eight systems of weapons or means of destruction have been given; the first three "conventional", the other five "weapons of mass destruction". (A weapon system would then include logistics and weapons carriers.) For each class of weapons there is a corresponding list of destructive agents or action. Thus, the weapons in the first class, piercing/impact, penetrate and crush. The incendiary weapons operate by means of flames, heat-flux and oxygen consumption. The chemical weapons (including toxins) work with their toxic effect, and the biological weapons by means of pathogenic microbes. The radiological weapons make use of radioactive substances. The nuclear weapons release energy as blasts (50%), thermal radiation (35%) and ionizing radiation (15%), initially and through fallout.[17] The geophysical or environmental weapons work through the release of latent energy in the cosmosphere (directed solar energy?), atmosphere (temperature and precipitation modification, hurricanes and typhoons, artificial lightning?), hydrosphere (tsunamis) and lithosphere (activating earthquakes and volcanoes, landslides and avalanches) and the biosphere (wildfires). And there are the possible new weapons: laser, particle beams, infra-sound, microwaves.

To understand the dynamics of military systems it is useful to make a distinction between *actio-reactio* dynamics between (usually opposed)[18] military systems, often called an arms race, and the *Eigendynamik,* whereby the system generates its own momentum. Both approaches, however, are too much focussed on the military systems alone and fail to take into account the broader social context in which they are embedded. Thus, military systems are after all related to conflict formations, within and between countries, which have to be taken into account to understand the dynamics. Moreover, they are embedded in macro-societies that undergo certain processes, developmental or not, and the military systems may have to adjust in order to be *structurally compatible.* Thus, if there is a basic change in the structure of the macro-society there is a limit to how long the military system may remain unchanged and vice versa: the military system may lead, not lag, behind the general social change – again in the direction of development or not. This underlies the theory of the military as an engine of development.

Obviously, it would lead too far to enter into this so the discussion will be limited to the *Eigendynamik* aspect. Three processes are usually emphasised, at least as hypotheses.

The preparation cycle hypothesis:

> Once a production cycle is started (with research) there will be strong intranational forces (MBCI complexes) pushing towards deployment, and international forces pushing further on towards proliferation.

There is also a hypothesized relation between the first three components, doctrine-organization-manpower and the production cycle, the next six. The first three may demand the production of a new military product. But the product may also be produced because it is *possible* to produce it, and to use idle production capacity, leading to a rationale: a change in doctrine, a change in organization or a change in humanpower composition. The strong interconnections in these chains and cycles make the system particularly resistant to efforts towards limitation, even control. Like a mature ecosystem its resilience is based on diversity and feedback loops – and it often has both.

The preparation-action cycle hypothesis:

> One tends to lead to the other.

The thesis that action leads to preparation is trivial; preparation follows from the depletion of military stock due to action. The thesis that preparation leads to action is not trivial, and not necessarily true either. Given that arms do not last forever it boils down to assigning probabilities to the four possible ways in which arms may disappear: by being *used,* by being *unwilfully destroyed* (attrition), by being *wilfully destroyed,* and by *proliferation* (trade/aid), entering some other military system. Wilful destruction is probably the least likely,[19] and in such cases the arms are usually replaced with more destructive arms. Costly products are not easily destroyed. There may be one important exception to this: *after a war* costly weapons not expended in the war may be destroyed, but then there has been a war! But there is a fifth possibility, sometimes: *civilian conversion,* swords into ploughshares, the most hopeful category.

The action cycle hypothesis:

> There will be escalation from less to more destructive weapons systems as action evolves.

The hypothesis is certainly valid historically as the list of eight classes of weapons systems – three conventional and five of mass destruction – already indicates. The process may also be reproduced at the level of the individual war (like phylogenetic development having some parallels at the level of ontogenetic development), for instance with escalation from conventional to nuclear wars. But the opposite may also be imagined: a first strike nuclear attack resulting in a general level of primitivization/brutalization so high that the war is continued with clubs; an impact weapon (the Einstein hypothesis).

The net conclusion from these three hypotheses is not pleasant to contemplate: preparation leads to more preparation, which leads to action, which leads to more destructive action. If this hypothesis were 100% valid humankind would probably already have ceased to exist. But if it were 0% valid we would not have had accelerating military preparation and increasingly devastating wars either. It is hard to attribute figures but the level of validity seems to be closer to 100% than to 0%.

To justify this assumption the *Eigendynamik* hypotheses about the internal dynamics of the military system of one party would be insufficient. If one adds the *actio-reactio* principle to the analysis of the preparation one gets a vicious circle operating between the two parties in the form of efforts to eliminate lags and perhaps establish leads in the components, both quantitatively and qualitatively. In military action escalation to more devastating arms is readily understood as a response to the other party. In addition to this the conflict formations in the world harden rather than soften because economic and bureaucratic cycles intersect, often cooperatively but also very often in conflict, become more extensive and denser without basic underlying conflicts being solved, usually conflicts between dominant *and* dominated, within *and* between countries. And structurally the military system is so similar to the organizations used for "development", bureaucracies and corporations, that they easily follow in their wake or lead the way – as a reserve, shadow society – which goes far to explain the many military coups and semi-coups. In short: a system in rapid, even uncontrolled growth.

2. First order effects of military activity

2.1. On war scenarios

We do not know what a future major war might look like. To stick to the war of major concern, a nuclear war: the total yield is said to be around 20,000 Mt, or about 1.5 million Hiroshima bombs (about 13kt).[1] Some scenarios operate with about half of this detonated, the other half being destroyed or unused. But it is not only a question of yield, but also of the height above ground zero, wind and other atmospheric conditions. From a social point of view the density of the population around ground zero is crucial, which is to some extent correlated with whether the attack is primarily *counter-force* (meaning against M (the military system) in the present scheme of analysis, and more particularly against all aspects of M relevant to nuclear warfare) or *counter-value* meaning against D (the development system) and to a lesser extent E (the environment). Since E and D on the one hand and M on the other hand are spatially mixed, whereas most effects of an explosion, including nuclear explosions, are spatially continuous, and even a small bomb has a big effect, this distinction may not always be so meaningful.

This becomes evident when one studies the estimated damage to D (e.g. to population and production capacity) under counter-force assumptions. Pure countervalue attack is meaningless, since it leaves retaliatory capacity intact. Damage can probably be reduced with dispersion of production facilities – a dispersion, it must be added, that would increase damage. And their hardening (difficult to do for agriculture, though) would turn society into an underground caricature. Moreover, it might also inspire a new generation of smaller, highly penetrating arms with homing devices. Damage to population may be reduced though the population equivalents, evacuation and sheltering (civil defense)[2] but both presuppose warning, which may be non-existent, *or* a permanently evacuated/sheltered population which means that society has, in a basic sense, already been damaged. Add to this possibility of hitting or not hitting nuclear power plants and nuclear waste disposals – making the fallout even more long-lasting and pernicious.[3]

In short, the uncertainties are many as to the effects of an attack. And this also applies to the two dimensions of time and space. In most scenarios there seems to be an underlying assumption that there will be a short, sharp shock. Much more likely, one might think, would be attack–interval–attack–interval–attack, to let the effects of the attack accumulate, letting people try to cope and to negotiate, and then a new attack. There is no good reason why a nuclear war should be short. The impact of such a dispersion in time seems hard to overestimate; protracted warfare leaving time for more accuracy.

As to space, the focus is on the northern hemisphere for nuclear war, among other reasons because all nuclear powers so far are in this hemisphere and this is also where the centers of the conflict formations are located.[4] There are some scattered targets in the South, but nothing like the NATO-WTO area, and inside them the likely targets for counter-force and/or counter-value approaches. The latter approach would definitely indicate the center rather than the periphery of the NATO-WTO land mass. But it is also hard to conceive of a counter-force attack that would not include centers of command also located in the urban centers. And even if the first strike is counter-force the second is likely to be counter-value, by doctrine and/or by spontaneous reaction to the damage wrought. But then again we do not know any of this. What will happen is guesswork – fortunately. Solid data would be the result of the war we must not have.

More precisely, we do not know what the scope of a war would be (extent of the destruction) or the domain of the war (area of destruction). The *worst* possible case, irreversible destruction (to be defined later), all over the world, seems still to be impossible.[5] The best case is easily defined – the best case being no war at all – and an even better case would be active, cooperative peace.

In between is the distinct possibility of a high level of destruction in the urbanized part of the NATO-WTO complex, with collateral destruction of neighboring areas and precise destruction of weapons sites. Hence this is the kind of war one can imagine. However, this image is Euro-centric. A major war might not only start in the Third World (as many scenarios will have it) but also end there, and yet include a nuclear confrontation. And it might be limited to a US/USSR exchange. There is no way of knowing.[6]

With all these qualifications let us then try to list first order effects of military activity on environment and development. But before that, a statement on a basic assumption, or rather lack of assumption, underlying the present analysis. As said above nobody knows what the *scope* (measured in megatonnage) or the *domain* (measured in area affected) of a possible nuclear war would be. In saying this we are implicitly rejecting two possibilities that to some people seem to be obvious truths: that a nuclear war can be kept very limited (e.g. only a warning shot) or will necessarily be unlimited, escalating in all ways, from powers to superpowers from the very beginning, from short range/low yield weapons to long range/high yield weapons, from some central area in the NATO-WTO system to the whole world. The extremes here should be accorded relatively low probability. Just as it would be unlikely to stop after a very limited exchange, or no nuclear exchange at all, so it would be as unlikely to go all the way in an insatiable rage for retaliation, completely heedless of the destruction wrought. For one thing, the capacity to go on fighting may be destroyed before eighter side runs out of bombs – among other reasons because the people "pushing the buttons" may be more concerned with saving their own families than killing those on the other side.

The highest *a priori* (and may it remain *a priori*) likelihood should be given to middle range possibilities. The analysis given in this text is of this kind. Thus, it assumes many dead, but also many survivors (although with lower life expectancy due to cancer). To accuse an author who believes there will be survivors of being "soft on the bomb" is already a sign of how deeply military worst case analysis has affected people. The military need this kind of absolutism, for if there are survivors then the question arises of whether they may possibly benefit from wiser foreign policies, such as neutrality/non-alignment. But many antimilitary also seem to feel a need for total apocalypse lest people should start getting more ready to accept a bomb that is comparable to the accumulated natural catastrophes thoughout history. We see no need to be steered by such considerations, and have consciously chosen a middle course. Even so, the outcome is more than bad enough.

2.2. Impact on the environment

We have a division of military activity into preparation and action and a division of the environment into six spheres (with subdivisions). Where are the key impacts located? Sticking to the language of environmental discourse the impact may be seen in terms of depletion and pollution to start with, except that instead of "depletion" the term often used is "diversion". This is an unfortunate usage in that it prejudges the issue: it builds into the vocabulary the notion that the natural (and other) resources used could be better spent, e.g. on development, or not spent at all, recuperating or being reserved for the future. This conclusion can only be justified by not only showing that the security doctrine underlying the military preparation is less valid than some other security doctrine, but *also* that the depletion differs according to the two doctrines that could be referred to as diversion. But such attempts are generally not made. To assume that all military preparation is diversion is to assume that *any* military preparation is irrational – which is an assumption so dramatic that it at least calls for a justification.

The most important depletion/pollution aspects of military preparation seem to be as indicated in Table 4. Of key significance is one trivial but important circumstance: military hardware is, as the term indicates, based on mineral resources and they are non-renewable. Weapons systems based on small arrows dipped in poison – e.g. *curare* – blown out through a hollow reed would not have this effect. The military system is a major consumer of fossil fuels and other scarce mineral resources[7] and an important consumer of land and water for testing and maneuvers.[8] That all this activity is associated with opportunity costs goes without saying: even if the land and water areas are marginal (which they are not necessarily), other uses for them can be imagined. And with the increasing size and sophistication of the military the need for land will increase, particularly for land away from cities.[9]

No impact of military preparation on the cosmosphere can be seen so far, except littering of outer space with satellites.[10]

The pollution aspect has been seen in the usual terms of air and water pollution, soil destruction and possibly also biota destruction. In addition to this comes the category of space littering. It is not obvious that the military as such pollute more or less than others. Being a hier-

Table 4. Military preparation impact on the environment[11]

	COSMOSPHERE	ATMOSPHERE	HYDROSPHERE	LITHOSPHERE	BIOSPHERE	HOMOSPHERE
Doctrine						
Organization						
Humanpower						people use
Research						people use
Development/ testing	littering	pollution	pollution water use	pollution; land use; soil destruction	pollution biota destruction	noise; health injuries
Production/ stockpiling		pollution	pollution	non-renewable minerals; fuels		
Training/ maneuvers			pollution; water use	non-renewable fuels; land use; soil destruction		noise
Deployment	littering			land use; possibly soil destruction		
Proliferation						

35

archical organization with strong emphasis on discipline, once the leadership have accepted rules about pollution they may enforce the rules. But they may also not accept them, and even feel it important to demonstrate that they are above the rules. The real analytical problem, however, is what is meant by the "military as such".

If the military sector were totally removed, or even if it were partially reduced, polluting industrial production (chemical, steel, metals in general) would be much reduced. If we assume a relation between capital and research intensity and pollution, and between military production and capital and research intensity, this conclusion should be not only valid but also more so than for the removal of many other sectors.[12] But there is an important flaw in the reasoning: it presupposes that there will be no conversion of these industries for nonmilitary purposes. The making of steel and the use of steel will pollute whether the end product is a tank or a tractor, the latter-day versions of swords and ploughshares. Whether it pollutes more or less is probably a marginal question, particularly as conversion, in order not to create too great shocks in the economy, would have to have to have approximately the same capital, labor, and research intensity as the military production it supersedes. And it may even not supersede military production at all if a transarmament rather than disarmament model is used. The conversion would be from offensive to defensive preparation rather than from military to civilian production. In short, in the production process we are faced with a *general* pollution problem, not necessarily a military one.

But even if, in general terms, the military do not pollute more than others in peacetime (and in wartime the rules do not count), there are some very important special aspects of the military preparation process that nevertheless fall under this heading – only they are not necessarily found in the production link of the chain. This will be explored in Chapters 4 and 5. As Table 4 indicates they are in the development/ testing and training/maneuvers in cosmos, air, land and water, including supersonic aircraft (ozone layer) and submarines (radioactivity). The areas involved can become considerable and so can the destruction. At this point it is difficult or impossible to invoke a civilian conversion equivalent with the same demand for non-productive use of surface area. If, however, a transarmament rather than disarmament scenario is used it is obvious that a purely defensive military system would also have a land need for development/testing and for training/maneuvers, although possibly not of the same size, since the weapons might be more static/

short range. On the other hand, the need for land for deployment might be even higher if the idea is to make the country "indigestible" at as many key points as possible. But there would not be "forward deployment", i.e. bases. And there might be less need for border zones, as the defense would be more in depth.

Turning to the impact of military *action* on the environment, the whole scheme of analysis becomes more complex. There are the same six spheres, and eight different classes of weapons systems. However, the exploration here will be focussed on nuclear weapons. This is as far as weapons systems go a worst case analysis. The effects of nuclear weapons include, directly or indirectly, most of the effects of the other systems – although there are some specificities of biological and chemical weapons to be taken up later, and some special aspects of the geophysical weapons. The simplest method is to proceed sphere by sphere, and for each sphere rank the components in terms of level of robustness/vulnerability. And here the general rule is clear: *biota are more vulnerable than abiota (in general), and the "higher" biota more vulnerable than "lower" biota* (quotes are used because one might also have said that "higher" should stand for more, not less robust; otherwise the terminology is standard).

Cosmosphere. So far direct destructive impact of military action on the cosmosphere has not appeared, apart from all the space junk that will increase enormously in a war. But there is a major impact on what the cosmosphere yields, through changes in the energy composition that reaches us through the atmosphere, decreasing the light and heat through dust formation and increasing the influx of ultra-violet radiation through depletion of the ozone layer caused by catalytic effects of nitrous oxides on O_3. There is also the possible creation of an electro-magnetic pulse, changing the electro-magnetic environment in a way highly destructive of electronic equipment.

Atmosphere. The general pollution of the air through radioactive fallout, the depletion of oxygen in firestorms, and neutron radiation creating carbon 14 out of nitrogen, with a long half-life, are among the effects. About climatic changes we probably know nothing.

Hydrosphere. The general pollution of water everywhere through radioactive fallout, carried through the hydrological system, coming down with precipitation, ultimately reaching the ground water.[13]

Lithosphere. Soil destruction through major physical impact (blast); craterization, etc., particularly on (steep) slopes.

Biosphere. The following is meant as a rule-of-thumb:[14]

ANIMALS: most vulnerable
humans (lethal dose 1/2 kR)
birds, mammals (1 kR)
reptiles, amphibians (2 kR)
insects
large more than small;
pre-, post-natal more than grown up,
domestic more than wild

PLANTS: very vulnerable
conifers (lethal dose 2 kR)
hardwood (10 kR)
grassland, prairie (20 kR)
tropical rain forest (40 kR)
herbaceous non-grasses (70 kR)
tundra (500 kR)
desert (already destroyed)
harvested more than crops;
rye more than wheat and corn more than rice;
tomatoes, beans, onions, lettuce very vulnerable

MICRO-ORGANISMS:
least vulnerable, in general terms.

In addition to these effects from radiation there is also the fire hazard.

Homosphere. The following is meant as a rule-of-thumb.[15]

HUMANS:
women slightly more vulnerable than men
younger (below 10) and older (above 40) more
than middle-aged
prenatal (foetus) and post-natal (infants) more vulnerable

HUMAN SETTLEMENTS:
houses less vulnerable than humans (to radiation)
bigger settlements more vulnerable than smaller
ones
– more likely as targets (counter-value)
– more disruptive chain-effects, etc. (see 3.2)

Whether on top of all of this there are also genetic mutation effects is not so clear. What is clear is that many effects are delayed, like cancers with gestation periods up to 40 years. Radionuclides have a continuous although decreasing delayed effect; delayed bombs a discontinuous one. And in addition to this there are blasts and fires.

To give a more complete survey the other weapons systems can be brought into the picture together with the nuclear system, as in Table 5 (see page 40).

Looking at the table as a whole one sees a clear movement through time from aggression against human beings only, highly species specific, towards the geo-physical *aggression against the environment,* which indirectly, of course, will hit human beings (unless they are well protected against exactly that type of assault).[17] Nuclear weapons cover all aspects, they are precisely *omnicidal,* changing and destroying everything. But that does not mean that high explosives cannot also cause soil disruption, directly through craterization and indirectly by eliminating the protective cover of vegetation and then destroying soil through erosion. Or, by breaking through to the water table, causing excessive evaporation and general disruption of the hydrological cycle. And incendiary weapons can be used for area denial, burning grassland as in the Boer war and the Second Indochina war. Toxic chemicals and biological weapons (based on harmful micro-organisms) can be used for deforestation/defoliation, as herbicides – and when used in areas with fragile soils, semi-arid areas may be pushed towards desertification – a process that seems to be difficult to reverse. A particular chemical weapon, napalm, also has this effect of removing sheltering forests and destroying crops. Nerve gases, on the other hand, are more species specific, as are, in general, biological and chemical weapons.[18]

Geophysical weapons suffer from the disadvantage that they may be difficult to direct. In the Table they appear as the opposite of the highly directed piercing/impact weapons, traditionally not only focussed on the human species but on specific human individuals. They are based on unstable equilibria in the environment (e.g. tectonic instability) whereas the ABC weapons are based on ecochains, using them to convey lethal effects. They are indeed macro-weapons as opposed to the micro-weapons used in earlier phases of human history and may be camouflaged as natural phenomena – causing the suspicion that natural phenomena are in fact directed weapons.

Table 5. Military action impact on the environment[16]

	COSMOSPHERE	ATMOSPHERE	HYDROSPHERE	LITHOSPHERE	BIOSPHERE	HOMOSPHERE
Piercing/impact					destructive of forests	destructive of humans
Incendiary		pollution			destructive of crops and forests, animals and plants	destructive of humans and settlements
High explosives		pollution	dyke destruction, floods	soil destruction, craterization	destructive of crops and forests, animals and plants	destructive of humans and settlements
Chemical/toxic		contamination	contamination	soil contamination	destructive of plants and animals	destructive of humans
Biological		contamination	contamination	soil contamination	destructive of plants and animals	destructive of humans
Radiological		contamination	contamination	soil contamination	destructive of plants and animals	destructive of humans
Nuclear	major changes	contamination, dust, ozone layer EMP effect, C^{14}	contamination	major soil destruction	highly destructive of all higher forms of life	highly destructive of humans and settlements
Geophysical	major changes	hurricanes lightning ozone layer holes climate in general	tsunamis ocean currents	earthquakes landslides avalanches volcanoes	generally destructive	generally destructive

Two conclusions emerge from the table. Humans are the key target – of course; wars are between humans. And the distinction between conventional and mass destruction weapons, especially nuclear, is basic.

2.3. Impact on development

The impact of military activity on the ten aspects of development defined in Table 2 will also be studied by first exploring the impact of military preparation, then the impact of military action.

The impact of military preparation is outlined in Table 6. It should be compared with Table 4 as they are to some extent complementary: the aspects of military preparation that play an important role in connection with the environment are less important in connection with development, and vice versa.

By and large there are two types of impact, what one might call *militarization* and what one might call *opportunity costs*. The former is a question of a certain explicit doctrine, implicit mentality and structure penetrating from the military system into the development system. The latter is a question of the military system consuming resources (not natural; they were considered in 2.2) such as capital and humanpower that could have been used for the purposes of development.[19] In the table military doctrine is seen to have an impact on human development by turning "identity" more towards military values (e.g. very strong ingroup identification, "nationalism"; and correspondingly strong hatred of outgroup); by reducing "freedom" for instance under the formula of protecting security; by subordinating other institutions in society to military goals and processes[20] (the MBCI complex, the military with bureaucracy-corporation-intelligentsia in tow); by generally reproducing itself in very vertical and large structures; and by penetrating the deep culture of society. And military organization is seen to reinforce this through its structure, just as the humanpower does so through the mentality inculcated in it. Secrecy is the opposite of participation. Military preparation will always be at the expense of structural development when it is based on secrecy.

The opportunity costs are measured in material basic needs units (BNUs) not realized because of military consumption of resources (capital, labor, researchers, research facilities, production facilities), which compete with production for development goals.[21]

Table 6. Military preparation impact on development[22]

	Survival	Wellbeing	Identity	Freedom	Production	Distribution	Institution	Structure	Culture
Doctrine			militar-ization	militar-ization			military	military	militar-ization
Organization		capital; opportunity costs	structure military	structure military	capital opportunity costs		military	structure military	
Humanpower		numbers opportunity costs	mentality military	mentality military	numbers; opportunity costs				mentality military
Research		opportunity costs			opportunity costs				
Development/ testing									
Production		opportunity costs			opportunity costs				
Training/ maneuvers									
Deployment									
Proliferation								structural transformation	

It should be noted that in a definition of "development" where basic needs do not appear, or not so prominently, this point would be missed. Military production would be seen as a contribution to GNP measured by market prices, and the arms market is the second biggest commodity market in the world, after oil. This point is also reflected in the idea of proliferation as the transfer mechanism of this particular MxD structure into another society, whether it distorts that society through secondary production or through trade, thereby influencing its trade structure. In either case the impact is considerable.

The whole argumentation is not unproblematic, as pointed out in the corresponding part of the preceding section. One should only legitimately talk about opportunity costs if the opportunity is lost in the sense that one is free to choose otherwise. To show this, the security doctrine justifying the military preparation has to be shown to be either totally false in the sense that there is no security problem at all, except the problem created by such a high level of military preparation, or to be inferior to an alternative security doctrine that absorbs less resources. The opportunity cost would be the difference between conventional and alternative military resource consumption, not the total military resource consumption. Again, it all depends on whether one's vision is the disarmament or the transarmament paradigm.

Something of the same can be said about militarization. It is a negative impact according to the goals of development defined in Table 2; for instance it generally implies neither self-reliance nor equity but rather dependence on a superpower. But what if the alternative is total loss of all developmental goals through enemy attack, victory and occupation? The costs of a course of action have to be evaluated relative to the costs (and benefits) of alternative actions. And if that alternative action is not disarmament but transarmament in all likelihood some measure of militarization (probably not that much) would be required also in that case.

There is a particular aspect of the militarization of the human personality/character – the effort to search for identity with something and to build space for freedom within oneself – that should be mentioned explicitly. Military preparation probably has an impact on the human mind in the form of *mental preparedness for violence*. For the military professional this is not an unmixed evil; it is after all preparation for the situation that calls for his skills. For the non-military it may come so close to an unmixed evil that the preparedness leads to forms of anxiety, fear, depression, even apathy, a fatalism in front of a danger so threatening, so massive and so seemingly unavoidable that it is suppressed in order to dampen and quiet the fear. If this is true it should already have affected a very large number of people – in fact so many that they/we may not be aware of it. The consequence would be low ability to deal rationally with the threats of military activity, preferring to try to forget about it all. One may, perhaps, try to rely on people in other parts of the world less affected by the military preparation. But then they may have other equally important problems to cope with, using the mechanisms of psychological escape available to human beings. The victim of all this escapism is above all the ability to find constructive alternatives.[23]

Finally, some words about the possible positive contributions of the military system to development. There is no doubt that from the military system also flow positive inputs to the development system; such as concrete innovations and products in the fieds of communication/ transport (aviation, ground transport, electronics in general). Nor is there any doubt that the military as an institution can satisfy the well-being needs for food, shelter, etc. and also many of the identity needs – even at the expense of both freedom needs today and survival needs tomorrow. But if one is sceptical about the opportunity cost argument the same applies to this "opportunity benefit" argument. The military may have been a sufficient condition for these inputs (as it is for the resource consumption), but not a necessary condition. Hence the argument should not rank high.[24]

Turning to the impact of military *action* on development, the whole scheme of analysis becomes more complex. For the same reason as in the preceding section we shall start with some of the key effects of nuclear weapons on development, and proceed dimension by dimension through the development system. Again the components within these dimensions or aspects could be ranked in terms of robustness/ vulnerability. The general rule is relatively clear and just the same as the corresponding rule for the environment: *the "higher" the level of development as conventionally conceived of, the lower the robustness* (quotes again because one might ask the question: what is so "high" about it if it is that vulnerable?).[25]

Any description of the possible impact of a nuclear war on the human and social fabric is bound to be speculative and controversial, not only in terms of effects postulated, but also in terms of the dimensions chosen for the analysis. And yet it has to be done; the possible consequences of human action in this field have to be seen clearly and understood in order to be counteracted. "Understood" means neither belittling them nor resorting to that analysis-killer "if a nuclear war breaks out we shall all die anyhow so it doesn't matter".[26]

Survival. We shall not all die; it obviously does matter where we live *geographically* (northern or southern hemisphere), *socially* (center or periphery, with some exceptions), *politically* (in the NATO-WTO system or not), and *topographically* (plains versus mountains). All these three dimensions should be seen as continua rather than as dichotomies. The numbers are staggering. An attack of 167 Mt on 188 targets in Britain is calculated to cause 6–8 million deaths and 10–16 million seriously injured; after one month perhaps 20 million killed.[27] A 300-Mt attack on the USSR with 300 1 Mt warheads and bombs will place 75 million of the population and 62% of the industry "at risk"; 300 warheads and bombs against the US with around 150 Mt will cause 40 million casualties and destroy 25% of the industry.[28] The US Office of Technology Assessment study operates with considerable differences according to whether the attack is mainly counter-force or whether it also has an increasing number of counter-value components. For the world as a whole one may realistically think in terms of 500 to 1000 million killed, or upwards of 10–20% of all humankind. The strategic weapons today are said to be capable of destroying 1.5 million km^2 if one calculates 15,000 warheads and bombs with almost 1 Mt as average yield, and destruction in non-overlapping circles of about 100 km^2 per Mt warhead/bomb. This is 3% of the land area of the NATO-WTO system and 1% of the world land area.[29] In calculations like this the effects of fallout are included, but not the possible destruction of the ozone layer because of the uncertainties surrounding this notion. If all 10,000–15,000 Mt are released in a war of many megatons, highly concentrated (big yield warheads), the impact on the ozone layer may be disastrous, it seems.

The figures are given here to make two points: *both* the tremendous destructiveness of a nuclear war in those parts of the world most likely to be the targets, *and* the fact that there will be surviving human beings and in all likelihood also surviving districts, countries and regions. It is with this type of reality one should try to explore the possible impacts of a nuclear war on development. Those who are unimpressed by the killing of "only" 10–20% of humankind[30] already betray disturbing signs of the mental degradation caused by the arms race.

Wellbeing. Given the differential impact of a nuclear attack on organic and inorganic material, food will be more destroyed than houses – as crops, but also as harvested stocks (depending on the degree of sheltering, of course). With water and air polluted the most basic needs will not be satisfied in hit areas, whereas somewhat less basic needs for comfortable, solid housing and transport/communication may be better satisfied since these are sturdier. An exception would be the impact of the electromagnetic pulse on transport/communication depending on electronic devices. In a sense this would recreate the situation in many developing countries: hunger amidst quite a lot of even impressive looking hardware such as cars, TV sets, stereos, if the latter are not also destroyed.[31]

But the fact that buildings are standing does not mean that the mechanisms inside them can function. Thus, it is generally assumed that health services will break down, dependent as they are on many vulnerable, highly diverse and interrelated components.[32] Schooling may perhaps break down less, being less complex as a system; but the struggle for food, water and air, for disposal of the dead and excreta, for sleep and basic reproduction will take priority over schooling. Everything will come down to basics, or to the most basic of the basics after a holocaust of this magnitude. It is *de*development in the extreme.

Identity. What kind of identity pattern will emerge after a nuclear attack? To start with positive identity will undergo a contraction towards self and social *micro*-space, family and peer groups. Over a little time identity with social *meso*-space, the local community and basic secondary groups (sex, age, race, ethnic, class, occupational groups), may re-emerge. But what about social spaces further out? Obviously the enemy who dropped the bombs will be hated. But that does not mean that one's own government will be loved, respected or obeyed. It may be profoundly blamed for not having conducted the politics that could have led to other results. In all Western countries in the NATO-WTO system the arguments against the current security doctrine are relatively well known among the population (even if not generally agreed with), and they will be remembered in this type of crisis and form a background for interpreting the events. The dead will have no say in the matter, but for the others it may not be obvious that the basic axiom of conventional security doctrine, *better dead than red/blue*,[34] is true. Many may blame their governments for having tipped the balance in the wrong direction, and/or for not having explored better policies that might have steered clear of either calamity. At the same time the macro-social spare will have broken down (probably most meso-spaces also), and the net result is likely to be a mixed feeling of rejection and irrelevance. And the same will apply to regional and global levels, and possibly also to identity with the transcendental except for the very strong believers, who will see the holocaust as God's punishment. But even for these and a few others there is little comfort to be derived in the long run from having predicted correctly.

For those who survive, the problem is not only one of extreme grief due to bereavement and anxiety about the survival of self and family/friends. This has occurred often in human history. Nor is it a question of rejection of a leadership rightly or wrongly blamed for not having averted the calamity – this may have been the case with many wars and also in connection with natural catastrophes (the government did not warn us in time, did not take precautionary measures; the catastrophe hit some more than others and those hit were not adequately helped/compensated, etc.). How to square this with the God of one's faith – in the NATO-WTO area the Christian God and the Idea of Progress from a humanist, liberal/capitalist or marxist/socialist point of view – is always problematic.

But in this case it goes still deeper. If Western civilization leads to self-destruction in addition to so much destruction of others, then there must be something basically wrong with the civilization itself, and not only with its Christian/liberal/marxist/humanist manifestations. This agonizing doubt about the whole basis of Western existence will be nourished by survival differentials in favor of the non-West, *grosso modo*, unless such differentials are eliminated through intended or unintended escalation in world space. More particularly, this doubt and accusation will be directed against the institutions of science and politics, but presumably also against more basic aspects, particularly as most parts of these societies are somehow involved in the military preparation, and hence co-responsible for military action and its effects.

All of this will hit deeper than wounding the body and mind with somatic and mental trauma. It hits the spirit. *Human* existence itself,

47

not only *my* existence, will be in doubt. A general aura of meaninglessness will descend over the whole human enterprise, creating a very
negative situation indeed for reconstruction.

Freedom. That movement in social macro space, the country as a
whole, will be controlled/impossible goes without saying. But the same
may apply to movement in meso (local) space because of external destruction and radiation danger. Being restricted to the shelter (in most
cases after the attack, not before because of lack of warning with the
current security doctrines) is an extreme limitation to micro space, a
fragmentation of society into very basic units. The condition is likely to
last for a long time and probably also to be habit-forming. This may
lead to a rebirth of the family and the peer group, but also to a hatred
of micro space as a source of extreme agony, at the same time as meso
and macro spaces are blocked.

Under such conditions people may compensate, to some extent by
internal mobility, psychic mobility, through fantasies, even creative activity. However, given what has been said above about the mental condition of the survivors it seems highly unlikely that this will happen to
more than a lucky few – those who even under concentration camp
conditions can become creative. It is seldom under the Hobbesian condition of "nasty, brutish and short" that the search for the life dimensions of being/becoming, identity and freedom, leads to human growth
and development, with a spillover in the form of an externally visible
creativity that can also enhance the life of others.

Production. Production is a problem of *means* of production – in the
primary and secondary sector of goods and the tertiary sector of services – and the *products* themselves, the goods and the services. It is
also a problem of inputs in the form of factors of production, and a
distributive machinery that will connect the output with the consumers.

If we now assume that (1) organic matter is more vulnerable than
inorganic matter and (2) human settlements are more likely to be destroyed the higher their order of magnitude, because that is where
both value and force (with some exceptions for the latter) are mostly
located, then the prospects are very bleak indeed. The means of production in the secondary and tertiary sectors are usually located in
cities, and given the density of urban grids much nuclear capability is

sufficiently close to cities for a counter-force attack to become a counter-value attack. This means destruction of factories, but also of firms – of banking and credit institutions, finance and insurance, the professions and in general of buraucratic and corporate centers of command[35] – except for the little that is relatively permanently sheltered together with (but for its survival preferably at a distance from) top military and internal order commands, the police.[36] What is not permanently sheltered cannot be assumed to survive, as has been mentioned repeatedly.

Not only the means of production, but also the factors of production will be hit, and not only in the sense that land, capital and labor will be destroyed. In addition their mobility will become drastically reduced because of the destruction of transportation/communication networks in the center (not so much at the periphery). Capital will not flow, labor will not travel; natural resources that have not been destroyed cannot be moved because of the destruction of petrol pipelines, for instance.

This does not mean that production in the countryside escapes unscathed, even though this may be true for small industries in the secondary and tertiary sectors that are well dispersed and built into local economic cycles. Primary sector production may not be directly hit, but (1) the biota are vulnerable to fallout, (2) the production in modern agriculture is very much based on industrial inputs that may no longer be available and (3) the products may not be edible because they will be directly contaminated (through fallout) or indirectly through contaminated air, water and nutrients, over time.[37] This is possible because plants are less vulnerable than birds and mammals (and humans). Which all amounts to saying that production will be reduced to something very rudimentary, manual, focussed on the most basic needs of the survivors, and certainly not necessarily able to meet even these.[38]

What has been said so far has focussed on the material aspects of production and products, known as the economic aspects. What about the non-material aspects? The means of production of culture are essentially humans, with their minds and hands, for writing, painting, playing, sculpturing, and these producers are as vulnerable as anyone else in the human settlements they have chosen or been compelled to live in. Their products are brittle or solid depending on the material. More often than not they are in cities, and more so the higher the order of magnitude of the habitat. Given this they are predestined for destruction to a large extent, world heritage treaties notwithstanding. Some cultural products may be put into shelters, meaning they disappear even before the war.[39] But that means that very concrete foci of identification, even pride in the whole human exercise in general, and the enterprise of cultural production in particular, will be removed from humanity. Reproductions elsewhere are not the same. A monument has something idiosyncratic about it, it is irreplaceable. And here the word "heritage" is important: with the removal of monuments and such artefacts in general, the ties with the past are also removed and a dangerous kind of alienation, a type of ahistoricity sets in, which will contribute even further to the general sense of the meaninglessness of existence.

What is true at the collective level is also true individually. A cemetery is a link, however tenuous, with ancestors, more important in some cultures than in others, unimportant in none. Already the high turnover of housing under normal conditions destroys links with the past, making the cemetry a last redoubt, so to speak. Remove this, and the individual is totally without roots in concrete, material reality. And for the artists or intellectuals in general who think that they may be granted an eternal life after this one, a non-transcendental afterlife so to speak in their artefacts – their paintings in museums and books in libraries – there is little comfort. Both museums and libraries are close to the centers of cities, i.e. close to ground zero. What will be left is a void, a socio-cultural vacuum.

Distribution. Some basic ideas about which categories on a world scale will be more or less hit have been given above. In general, categories of people will be hit in proportion to their size, but there are some important exceptions.

Can anything be said about the relative quality of victims and survivors of a nuclear war? Will the fittest survive, and who, then, are the "fittest"? By definition the best protected will stand the best chance of survival, but "best" relative to a nuclear attack means something accessible only to the few. Roughly they will divide into two groups: public persons (elites) given access to special protection because of their presumed importance for collective survival, and private persons, survivalists, who have made their own shelters for individual survival. In either case we are dealing with somewhat special types. They would have in common a sense of being apart from the rest of humanity, as evidenced by the willingness to seek ultimate shelter in face of a destruction that may well hit everybody else. They probably also have in common a self-perception of being the "best"– for the public persons because they have been selected for survival, although mainly by themselves (and with a preponderance of middle-aged men, probably with higher education), for the private persons because they have elected to survive and thereby demonstrated both motivation and capability.[40] From the outside they may both look somewhat alike: authoritarian and selfish, high on money and/or power but on little else. More likely than not they will be carriers of conservative, status quo-oriented values.

This already indicates that the benefit of survival, if it is a benefit, will not be enjoyed equally. The very central power-holders, and the very marginal at the periphery, protected by mountains and distance, will stand a higher chance of survival than others. Certain character structures, and not necessarily those most appreciated in democratic societies, will be rewarded by survival. But what the more precise demographic composition and psychological profile of the survivor population will be it is difficult to estimate, except that it will be socially polarized and probably more authoritarian.

Institutions. Institutions are concrete social arrangements dealing with specific, but also diffuse, social functions. Institutions are working arrangements that make societies last – to the benefit of some and the cost of others if the societies are very vertically structured.

The following institutions are particularly important:
micro space: family, peer groups, mixtures of the two
meso space: villages (vertical), communes (horizontal), mixtures
macro space: markets, plans, mixtures of the two; transportation/communication; religion/ideology; government
all spaces: self-reliance, including self-sufficiency in essentials; participation in decision-making concerning oneself
between spaces: federalism, meaning multi-tier decision-making, division of labor, election, accountability and recall for representatives

In the *world space* there are certainly institutions that would have been important, but none can be said to be successful; and those that are successful, e.g. imperialism and the arms race, we would be better off without.

What chance do these institutions stand in the face of a major onslaught? In extreme crisis macro society would probably become institutionally stripped. The self-reliance of the micro and meso spaces may be enhanced because of social disintegration. The macro space would become much less participatory, with no election, no accountability and recall. Any federalism would yield to national centralism, which, as mentioned, may not be able to reach into the corners of a disintegrated society.

Taking human history as a guide, the recovery time could be very long, not because it is so difficult to rebuild when there is a willingness to do so but because of the vested interests of the new centers emerging in the crisis, with the power to defend their interests against a weakened and probably also marginalized and fragmented population. It takes little time to replace a democratic order by an authoritarian one – a coup is enough. It may take decades, even generations, to reverse that process, it is so brutally asymmetric.

At the economic level, centralized leadership, under conditions of extreme scarcity, will have to operate with production plans and strict rationing. Such systems at the macro level will tend to be accompanied by markets at the micro and meso levels, seen by the authorities as "black" and by the participants as indispensable for survival, and as "green". In other words, economically speaking we also arrive at the conclusion of a dual system, maybe not so unlike the duality under which the populations in state socialist countries in Eastern Europe are used to living. This would be a point in their favor in case of a war of this kind: they have more training in survival under such conditions, and hence will be less vulnerable.

Under such conditions the government will tend to be military, and authoritarian/repressive, even in the extreme. They will probably try to place spies, informers, inside the small units. They will have to try to cope with conditions of extreme scarcity and a defiant, even rebellious population which may have serious doubts about the legitimacy of a government seen as being partly responsible for the crisis, yet not as sharing the costs, as evidenced by its use of shelter and dispersion techniques for survival for its own purposes. The disorganization of the social fabric is itself a type of destruction and the conditions for repair could hardly be worse. Decisions will be perceived by many as arbitrary and inequitable. Social cleavages along lines of sex and age groups, ethnic and racial divisions, class and district, are likely to be accentuated rather than bridged because people will become more, not less selfish and identify above all with themselves and their own groups. Processes towards authoritarian character formation will lead to tendencies to repression, submission, and rejection of everything that comes from the government. And the government will have to spend much of its time trying to justify itself – both its previous policies leading up to the crisis, and its day-to-day decisions.

Structure. There are many ways of conceiving of social structures. One way is in terms of whether *vertical* or *horizontal* relations dominate, another whether the structure is *big or small* in terms of the number of humans it comprises.[41] This gives us four possibilities out of which one is impossible: that there is an upper limit to the number of people who can relate to each other in a two-way manner, without marginalizing, fragmenting or segmenting the other persons:

	VERTICAL	HORIZONTAL
BIG	Alpha	Impossible
SMALL	Gamma	Beta

The terms are chosen so as to connote absolutely nothing, although it is obvious that the alpha structures are predominant in bureaucratic-corporate-military systems, beta structures in peer groups and some families and kinship systems, gamma in many families (with a *pater familias*), tribes (with chiefs), and that most systems are mixtures of them all. Thus, sociologists often point out that although in a bureaucracy, or in most organizations for that matter, the formal organization chart may look alpha, there is an informal parallel system where people relate to each other in a beta manner. The argument can be made that a completely alpha or completely beta society would be a bad society, and that a good society would be a proper mixture of the two.[42]

What is the likely impact of a nuclear war of some magnitude on social structure in general? Most probably a polarization of society into an extremely vertical, authoritarian alpha structure operated from a center safely sheltered and prepared in peace time, under martial law or similar rules on the one hand, and on the other scattered groups that take on gamma structures in face of the extremely harsh conditions they encounter. Such gamma groups may or may not be attached to the centralized alpha structure, depending on the power of the latter – in terms of its moral command, whether it has anything to offer (e.g. food) and whether it can carry out threats (e.g. capital punishment). But if the alpha structure is in possession of two or three of these types of power, then, given adequate transport/communication facilities, the likely result is a giant alpha structure. Such a society, organized like a very conventional military system, would be a tremendous step backwards in terms of social development, here taken in the sense of *structural* development. The same could be said if the result were a disintegration of society into a multitude of scattered gamma and beta structures, not only small but isolated, out of touch with a greater social reality and the social dialectic that comes about from contact between, and not only within systems. In short: *social degradation.*

The same reasoning applies to the impact a major attack has on the total world structure. This structure is today very much an alpha structure, characterized by being vertical (exploitative) and big (world-encompassing in political/military and economic systems) and for that reason highly dependency-creating. The destruction of the center of this world structure will thus have short-term negative impacts on the periphery – roughly speaking the Third World. But it serves no good purpose to disregard that the long term consequences *may* be positive for the periphery. They would get out of habit-forming ties of dependency and inequity, ties that have even become addictive, particularly to many Third World elites in the sense that they cannot do without them if they are to maintain their power and privileges. Of course such a "liberation" would not have been due to the strength of the periphery, but to the weakness, to the point of self-destruction, of the center, and for this reason not of the same quality in the long run. But one consequence, for instance, would be to force the Third World to be self-sufficient in food supplies, and to struggle for industrial self-sufficiency. At any rate, it would be highly unrealistic to believe that the general world balance could be the same after a major nuclear exchange. It is not social science fiction to think in terms of "massive transfer" from South to North afterwards for reconstruction[43]– except that the South is not rich enough to make it all that "massive".

There is, however, a part of the world located – both geographically and politically/economically – between the First and Second Worlds on the one hand (dominated politically by the NATO-WTO system) and the Third World on the other: East and Southeast Asia. This part of the world, with Japan at its center, surrounded by China, the "mini-Japans" (Korea, Taiwan, Hong Kong, Singapore) and some culturally not quite similar countries (Philippines, Thailand, Indonesia, Malaysia, Australia, New Zealand and Oceania in general) would probably retain considerable reconstruction capacity. However, being in the North, particularly Japan and China, and linked to the superpowers in their conflict formations, they may not emerge sufficiently unscathed to reconstruct others, not even themselves. But more likely than not their relative position, already very strong, will become even stronger, underlining even more the suicidal policy the two centers in the Occident, the superpowers, are engaging in. And also the danger that in a nuclear confrontation they may destroy Japan and China in the process – not as enemies, but to eliminate possible competitors after the war.

Culture. What effect will a war with weapons of mass destruction have on culture? One key hypothesis would be that it has a brutalizing effect, perhaps on the victims as well as, or even more than, on the perpetrators of such crimes. The latter may be shocked by the effect of their action into an "agonizing reappraisal", somewhat similar to what Germans went through when confronted with the horrors perpetrated on the world by the Nazi regime. But the victims will also go through an agonizing reappraisal, although it may well take place in the much deeper recesses of their minds, in the collective unconscious. The actors have to face their action subjectively, trying to come to terms with questions of responsibility, perhaps even guilt.[44] But the survivors among the victims have to struggle with the deeper problems of why they were the victims; with a diffuse sense of guilt rather than the agony of being the authors of atrocious acts. There is also the problem of what to learn; of what never more means in terms of concrete action, after a traumatic experience at that level.

The most likely conclusion drawn, although not necessarily at the conscious level, would be to imitate, even overdo what the perpetrator had done. Extreme violence would leave its imprint on the collective unconscious and spawn not only visions of revenge, but also serve as a nucleus around which a culture condoning extreme violence may crystallize.[45] Violence is reproduced through the violent act; a violent culture is transferred through the very act of violence A cultural code can also be transferred through colonialism, through language, religion,

55

technology (as materialized culture), but the violent act may be an equally potent transfer mechanism. Thus, after a nuclear holocaust the rhetoric will certainly be *Never More,* but the wounds deeper down may lead in another direction. The net result is likely to be a doctrine that "to prevent this from happening again we have to have even stronger weapons than ever before" – in other words the type of doctrine that emerged as a response to the First and then to the Second World Wars after the period of peace rhetoric was over. Nazi Germany drew this type of conclusion from the defeat of Germany in the First World War, but not in the Second – one could say. The United States, however, developed arms (nuclear) even worse in their implications than those the defeated Nazi Germany had used – because of Hitler, and Nazi Germany in general, the US felt that everything was permitted.[46] The Soviet Union responded in kind. The United States used weapons of mass destruction in the Second Indochina War;[47] there is hardly any doubt that it had a brutalizing effect on the Vietnamese. Vietnam may or may not have used weapons of mass destruction in Kampuchea.[48] But the extreme brutality of the Pol Pot regime may at least partly be explained by the extreme brutality to which Kampuchea was exposed in the Second Indochina War. And the brutality of the Israelis in Beirut by the holocaust in the Second World War. And so on, and so forth.

But there will also be those who draw the opposite conclusion from the *never more!* injunction. It will probably take the form of a total or partial rejection of basic tenets of Western civilization. The self-appointed position as the center of the world may be given up. The Idea of (material) Progress likewise. A science based on an atomistic/deductive approach may be seen as partly responsible for the crisis, and be replaced by anti-scientific or alternative orientations.[49] There may be scattered efforts to find, and justify, more egalitarian patterns of production and consumption in society. The relation to nature will have to be one of utmost care in a post-attack world of extreme scarcity; this may stick and become a part of the deep culture. And ideology/religion will definitely become less missionary, less universalist. There will be a widespread feeling that there is little to be proud of since the question will be, not of one part of the Occident defeating the other, but of two parts defeating each other and consequently the Occident in general – except for the Islamic part if this is counted as belonging to the Occident (as one of the religions of the Book).

56

This cultural polarization between those who want to build on the past in an extreme crisis and those who want to reject it will probably coincide with the social polarization alluded to above.

Nature. One condition for taking good care of nature is "enlightened self-interest": we shall live off nature today, and our offspring will to-morrow, so treat her well![50] Another condition would be some kind of empathy with nature, or at least nature as an object of admiration, even inspiration. A third condition would be to go still further and talk about love of nature in the sense of physical and spiritual intimacy, compassion, identity. But for this to emerge nature has at least to some extent to be lovable. A post-nuclear attack nature would not satisfy that condition. Degraded ecosystems do not look attractive. A craterized battlefield is ugly in the extreme. And in addition to all that meets the naked eye there is the invisible, inaudible, continuous insult to all live matter including humans: radiation. Consequently, it will only be among the deeply convinced that ecological thinking and ac-tion will be based on compassion for nature. And this compassion would be with a wounded and crippled nature that needs it far more than a nature consisting of a high number of mature ecosystems. Even today resources are not readily forthcoming to help build a stronger nature. There would be even less under the conditions described above.

*   *   *

Ideally one should now do the same exercise for the other seven weapons systems and then write out a table. However, this makes little sense since they differ more in their impact on the environment (see Table 5) than in their impact on development. In principle all other weapons systems are subsumed under nuclear weapons, which are the worst. All weapons systems can have the impact described above if applied to a sufficient extent. What is new about nuclear weapons is that they are all the other weapons wrapped into one and can do all this damage, initially in a matter of seconds; and finish it all off in a month or so. It all depends on the magnitude of the attack. Even a fraction of the destructive yield available today will have the impact mentioned above, according to the estimates, on some part of the world – how big a part depends on the yield and the spread. Hence there is little or no reason for filling in the table – the entries have already been made in the preceding text.

2.4. Some scenarios

If one now adds up Tables 4, 5 and 6 (and the table that was not spelt out, except implicitly in the text), military action is, of course, more destructive than military preparation; the homosphere is hardest hit; and nuclear weapons on the one hand, and radiological/geophysical weapons on the other, are the most destructive – also during preparation. About the impact of the "new weapons" we know very little.[51] The focus of interest is on nuclear war. And the story is easily told: the more vulnerable the target, the more destruction. Efforts to make oneself invulnerable are by and large ineffective, except safety through distance.[52] The more complex and differentiated, the more vulnerable. What remains would be small, scattered human habitats, microorganisms and insects, minerals. *Nuclear warfare is anti-evolution.* In the year of the Darwin centennial it is Darwin in reverse, only considerably quicker. There has always been this horrifying asymmetry between the time and energy it takes to create a mature human being and the split second and ease with which that miracle, the human life and consciousness, can be terminated. In this case it is not only one life but millions, not only humankind but life in general, not only the biosphere but other spheres as well. No wonder that theologians refer to the production, threat and possible use of nuclear weapons as "blasphemy". The destruction is at a level of magnitude that ought to be the prerogative of the Creator Himself. And yet the "flood" of the Bible seems moderate compared to a nuclear holocaust. From an environmental point of view the flood, as far as one can understand, was a clean operation, leaving cosmosphere, atmosphere and hydrosphere intact – and some of the lithosphere (such as Ararat). A nuclear war is not that considerate.

What went wrong? Nothing particular. All that happened was a completely logical consequence of the logic of the Second World War, and later development is a consequence of the security doctrines currently held by so many states. It is of no avail to lament the human mind or condition in general – they are not easily changed. If we want some basis for change some other approach is needed.

The approach taken here opens for a considerable number of approaches. Depending on which aspects of military preparation and action one focusses on (quality aspect), and up to what level of consumption and destruction (quantitative aspect), different impacts on environment and development can be envisaged. The mode of analysis does not presuppose worst case, best case, or any other particular case analysis. More particularly, there would be no built-in assumption to the effect that a war escalates in scope until the whole arsenal of weapons of mass destruction in general, and nuclear weapons in particular, are exhausted, or in domain until the whole world is a battlefield. The present author, as mentioned above, inclines to disbelief in either extreme. It seems unlikely, for instance, that some negative feedback would not come into play much before exhaustion of the nuclear arsenals. Such speculations are not entirely unimportant in a search for *action today,* because the action to try to prevent a drift towards nuclear war, or to reduce the impact by making societies less vulnerable to an attack through civil defense, depends on one's image of the range of likely scenarios. Much has been said about the danger of belittling the impact of nuclear attack through visions of "limited war" (in scope and/or domain, e.g. tactical weapons in Central Europe) and some civil defense measures – it probably breeds a callous attitude and lowers the threshold so that a nuclear war becomes a more likely outcome when/if a conflict develops into a confrontation.

But something more should be said about the opposite scenario, that of complete and total destruction. Such apocalyptic visions are deeply embedded in the collective unconscious (the "cosmology") of the Occident (Armageddon); less so in other parts of the world. Scenarios along such lines, however, seem counterproductive. Instead of mobilizing for action they may lead to apathy – although we probably know little about the concrete effects of such visions. One particular reason for apathy would be the lack of incentive to be among the survivors if there will be no survivors anyhow. And this is not merely a question of being an *individual* survivalist among a population badly hit – that is obviously a question of where and how deep to hide in the world. It is also a question of how to become a *collective* survivor, a country coming out of the war relatively intact in a region badly hit, which is obviously a question of what concrete security policy to choose. Both the individual and collective survivalist need information or theories about the dimensions that condition survival so as to construct the optimal strategy. One cannot blame people for doing so – this is what rational behavior in the face of overwhelming danger is about. One may envy them, but that is something quite different.

Any gradient in the map of survival probabilities is a guide to concrete action at the individual or collective levels. The individual actions are fairly obvious and can be found in any civil defense manual – whether shelters offer sufficient protection, in the case of a likely scenario, to be worth one's while is another matter. More interesting is the collective level, because this gives the key to alternative foreign policies. Countries basing their foreign policy on possible use, even first use, of nuclear arms will have to come to grips with nuclear war as a potential reality. They will tend to overemphasize the likelihood of individual survival and underemphasize the collective survival chances that might come from a different foreign policy. And this is a question of *alternative security doctrine,* in Chapter 4; rarely discussed for the simple reason that it may challenge the deeper assumptions underlying much of contemporary military policy.

3. Higher order effects of military activity

3.1. Introduction

So far the effects of military activity have been discussed as if environment and development were mainly sets of spheres and lists of elements. But they are systems, meaning that there is interaction between these elements – such as, for instance, food chains or energy chains. More particularly, there are five kinds of links that are indispensable in exploring environment and development as systems: *chains, cycles, synergisms, composition* and *recovery* systems (see the appendix).

The more of such links there are, in general terms, the more differentiated and complex, the more diverse and impressive the production of the system – environmental or developmental. *But* – the more vulnerable the system. That is, it may overcome insults up to a certain point because of its resilience. The impact is absorbed. But if the impact is beyond this absorption capacity, then the system may suffer a rapid decline. The equilibrium is meta-stable like a bowl which contains a ball very well and brings it back to the bottom as long as the ball does not have sufficient energy to roll over the brim.

The conventional development system is vulnerable, among other reasons because of insufficient diversity in the sociotypes and because of excessive dependency on the chains. This carries over in its relation to the environment system in the form of monoculture of plants and animals and excessive pressure on the environment in general. There is little or no redundancy in the total system, no fallback system. The total system may degrade, even disrupt, with the removal of only a few components, particularly if the center is removed, or if the primary producers are removed, the latter being true both for environmental and developmental systems. The vulnerability is the price the system pays for its differentiation and the high material and nonmaterial production known as development. And that price may have to be paid if the extreme exercise in de-development known as nuclear war should be carried out.

3.2. Impact on the environment

(1) *Chains*. The word "chain" already conveys the point. The eco-systems on which humans depend because of their biomass production are chains; hence, any destruction brought in at any trophic level below humans in the food chain may trigger a chain effect. If humans are hard to find as targets, or culturally unavailable because of strong norms for political or moral reasons against direct killing, there is an indirect possibility through the destruction of food chains. However, the destruction has to be extensive in domain, and deep in scope, to be sure to hit. Local but complete destruction will only lead to migration, a reason why islands are vulnerable: there is nowhere to go. Widespread but superficial destruction may lead to too rapid recovery. Hence attacks have to be directed against the primary producers on a large scale (e.g. by means of "defoliants", herbicides, Roma ploughs, etc.). This goes far to explain the enormous scale on which various weapons systems were used in the Second Indochina War.[1] It was area denial in the shape of a war against the environment, with the ultimate goal of hitting the enemy. Even more lethal approaches would be through the introduction of radio-nuclides in eco-chains.

Thus, in "modern" warfare eco-chains are used systematically to magnify the impact of an attack, by destroying primary producers, even destroying inputs to primary producers. If in addition one managed to destroy some of the many micro-organisms that do their work to make the systems function, e.g. as reducers turning biota into abiota again, the whole system will collapse. We are not quite there, yet. It is enough to take the forests as an example. Destruction of forests means not only destruction of primary producers, and thus food-chains, but also elimination of a basic source of fuel for heating and cooking (about half of the fuel comes from forests); of building material, e.g. for houses; of raw material for paper so crucial in communication; and as the basic factor protecting eco-systems against soil destruction through erosion.

In general one may say there are two approaches here: killing humans *by poisoning,* transmitted through the eco-chains, and *by killing* the eco-chains.

(2) *Cycles.* In a sense even more to be feared in this context than the chains are the cycles, because of the self-reinforcement brought about through positive feedback mechanisms. In principle cycles can be virtuous or vicious depending on whether or not one likes the final outcome; the focus here is on vicious cycles.

In the first type (see the appendix) *eco-system degradation would be self-sustaining.* Since the food chain is a part of an eco-cycle there is no difficulty in finding examples. Destruction of biota, e.g. forests, may lead to destruction of abiota through soil destruction, which leads to even more destruction of biota – in other words a clear case of a multiplier effect. This is one more reason why forests (and reforestation as a positive strategy) are so crucial[2] and thus of military significance. For the long-term effect it is worth contemplating the naked rocks on the Dalmatian coast, an effect of the Romans cutting forests to build their ships 2000 years ago.

In the second type *eco-system degradation would lead to more military action, which would lead to more eco-system degradation.* The secondary military action will perhaps not be so much over fossil fuels and other mineral resources as over uncontaminated water, land, perhaps also air if that is meaningful, so as to grow crops for basic sustenance, and have drinking water. In other words, the wars of history will be repeated, over primary resources rather than over secondary ones which enter as inputs for industrial production. The possibility of wars over women as breeders to compensate for demographic gaps at home should not be disregarded – after all this is also an ancient practice. In this sense as in so many others in this study of impact the future is to be found in the past. We may be living history in reverse, like reliving the Roman Empire, running out of resources, always having to go further out to satisfy our greed, even need.

It may be objected that with fewer humans around there will be less pressure on the resources, and with humans being among the most vulnerable biota the net balance after a war might even be more favorable. But this argument neglects the contamination that will take place and the vulnerability of humans to radio-nuclides that have entered the food chain in general. The struggle will be over *uncontaminated* resources, not just over resources. And they may be few and far between.

(3) *Synergisms*. These have been touched upon in the literature, main-ly in connection with nuclear warfare, and should become a very im-portant field of research. The approach would be to start with the de-structive agent or action on which a class of weapons is based, e.g. nu-clear weapons. However, in that case one might add to blast, thermal radiation and ionizing radiation two more agents triggered by initial energy releases: dust[3] and ultraviolet radiation. One could then start combining them two and two (or more), searching for possible syner-gisms – keeping in mind that the interaction effect might also be nega-tive, one agent cancelling some of the effect of the other. Some impor-tant hypotheses:

> *radiation + thermal burns:* plants killed through radiation burn better, which means more spread of the incendiary aspect of nuclear warfare.[4]

> *blast + thermal radiation:* the blast will trap humans and animals inside buildings and other structures so that they more easily become victims of fires.[5]

> *dust + ultraviolet radiation:* cooling of the atmosphere, hence fewer frostfree days and less possibility of growing wheat at higher latitudes.[6]

Correspondingly, one might speculate that the blast serves to de-stroy and topple in such a way that ionizing radiation obtains more access, if there is anything left to kill.[7] There may also be more to EMP than we know today. After all, the effect was only discovered afterwards; it was not intended, not even predicted.

(4) *Composition*. With the high differentials in vulnerability in natural eco-systems the surviving system will have a different composition as higher animals, lower animals and higher plants, and then lower plants are removed. The system will then find a new equilibrium given the improved situation for insects, lower plants and microorganisms with the biota that prey on them removed from the scene.[8] The point is not that the system cannot become stable again, even mature. But it will be different from the eco-systems to which humans have adapted in the past, and possibly even very hostile, with a higher incidence of pathogenic microbes, for instance, in search of hosts.

Then there are the nonnatural ecosystems based on the interaction between the other spheres and the homosphere. Houses and other artefacts may have a sheltering effect, so that domestic animals may survive when they are not out in the open – but this hardly compensates for the animals' lack of training on facing danger or for the fact that both they and the bombs will tend to be where the humans are. They may also get trapped. But animals below the ground, like moles and badgers, and rats in sewers and underground, may survive better than others.[9] They may serve as hosts to parasites with pathogenic microbes and breed uncontrolled, having no predators. On the balance biota enjoying this type of protection will probably be harmful rather than beneficial to man.

(5) *Recovery*. Where the primary producers have been killed and there is little migration into the area able to establish a pioneer community and engage in ecological succession (e.g. because the radiation is too hostile), the reducers will do the rest of the job, ending with mineralization and nitrification. The atmosphere composition will be tilted in favor of nitrogen and CO_2, away from oxygen. The hydrosphere may be less touched except that it can no longer be a habitat for biota who do not find enough nutrients and cannot stand the contamination. The lithosphere will lose its soil (humus) and desertification will set in. From that point on recovery seems to be extremely difficult even when aided by human inputs because of the hostile context (sandstorms, for instance). Under such circumstances energy from the sun can no longer be captured and packaged in a way humans can make use of.

Recovery rates for the other ecosystems are, of course, more favorable: decades for grassland (prairie), centuries for forests. For agriculture it may be less if the human inputs are available – the question is whether they are. Being generally very simple, monocultural systems they are already immature and low on natural healing power with no redundancy that can help towards restoration of maturity.

3.3. Impact on development

(1) *Chains*. Like eco-systems, social systems are (often, not necessarily) organized in chains of producers and consumers, where the output for one is the input (raw material, raw factors) for the other. Corresponding to trophic levels in eco-chains, there are levels of processing

in social chains, within communities, between communities within countries, and between countries. In general the lower levels can survive without the higher levels, but not vice versa. Hence, any destruction of the lower levels carries with it a destruction of higher levels that depend on the lower levels for food, raw materials, raw capital, raw labor (meaning unskilled), and so on. The more a society is hierarchically organized the more vulnerable it is in general. Of course, there is also some reciprocity in the chain: the higher levels contribute with decisions and usually monopolize relations with other systems.[10] If higher levels (cities, centers in general) are eliminated, the lower levels can often survive, but will have to find some new steering system and some ways of coping autonomously with the environment. One important point, to be explored later, is that, like eco-systems, social systems can change by cutting the chains through higher levels of local self-reliance, meaning reliance on the local environment and the developmental forces of the local community.[11] If this is difficult or even impossible, then the society is indeed vulnerable. But in general the "lower" levels can do better, since they are not preyed upon.

(2) *Cycles*. Using the same distinction as above (3.2) the first type would be the cycle where societal degradation brought about by military preparation or action would be self-sustaining. One important cycle would be based on the

$$\begin{array}{ccc} \text{authoritarian} & \rightarrow & \text{authoritarian} \\ \text{social structure} & \leftarrow & \text{character structure} \end{array}$$

loop, which can be activated by military preparation and/or by military action, and is crucial in running a thoroughly militarized society as such. Another loop would be:

$$\begin{array}{ccc} \text{material deprivation} & \rightarrow & \text{internal cleavages} \\ \text{through military} & \leftarrow & \text{with structural or} \\ \text{use or destruction} & & \text{direct repression} \end{array}$$

which can also be started at either end by preparation and/or action.

More clearly related to military action would be the way in which large-scale killing creates demographic imbalances that are pushed on to the next generations[12] (e.g. by radiation and malnutrition). Large-scale damage *in utero* and early infancy lead to mental deficiencies that will counteract higher production/productivity.[13]

In the second type of cycle *societal degradation would lead to more military action which would lead to more societal degradation*. The two cycles just mentioned could easily be extended in this manner: preparation leading to more authoritarian structures (both social and personal), leading to more preparation, and so on. This particular hypothesis becomes very important in connection with nuclear warfare. Among the survivors would be, probably, an over-representation of authoritarians, who had either selected highly authoritarian structures in which to work, or who had been formed by long tenancy in these structures. More concretely, they would be top level military officers, politicians, bureaucrats and corporate leaders, used to manipulating people at at distance, as objects rather than subjects. In addition the "survivalists" may represent a more populist version of the same inclination. By sheltering the top echelons (and making them the first to know when the danger is real so that they can prepare better than others for personal protection), society is in fact reproducing exactly those characteristics that may have produced the present unfortunate situation – like preserving the genetic stock of the maladapted rather than the adapted. After emerging from the shelters the chances are that they will do again what they did before, interpreting the bad turn of events as evidence that they had not done enough along those lines, not that the lines were wrong.

There is a particular cycle well worth paying extra attention to:

| Economic crises | → | Arms race to stimulate production War/destruction to stimulate production | → | Overproduction and new crisis |

Linking all this together one gets an endless chain of cycles: some types of maldevelopment leading to military preparation/action, leading to more maldevelopment and more military preparation/action. It is this kind of vicious cycle humankind somehow has to learn to turn into a virtuous cycle. It may be argued that we are already in this cycle today and have been for some time, and that we seem to have no learning capacity.

(3) *Synergisms.* They abound in this area as they are so characteristic of social reality. They may also be difficult to distinguish from chains and cycles. To take an example: military doctrine, mentality and structure, as they affect civilian society in the process known as militarization. Obviously they support each other, acting simultaneously rather than consecutively, a case of synergistic impact. Or take, under

67

action, the polarization (hypothesized) of institutions, structures and culture into a core that is an authoritarian version of the past, and peripheral parts that may also be authoritarian in their struggle to cope, but are at the same time in search of autonomy. These three processes of polarization will also support each other, leading to a total breakdown of the socio-cultural order as we know it into a core incapable of governing and peripheral fragments pitted against each other for survival.

(4) *Composition*. Every war kills selectively and hence will have some effect on the genetic pool. This also applies to nuclear war. The question is whether there will be other changes in the genetic code, not only in the distribution of the genetic codes – and, of course, whether the changes will be adaptive or maladaptive. By far the majority of them will be maladaptive, as typing errors usually are. But findings from Hiroshima-Nagasaki do not seem to indicate that there will be such changes.[14] The question remains whether one can generalize from this to heavier onslaughts on the human species. There is also the question of transmission of authoritarian social and personality structures in the upbringing of children by the survivors. As to sociotypes: small habitats will survive better, and will probably grow without being preyed upon by the larger ones, which will have more difficulty recovering.

(5) *Recovery*. The recovery rate is a question of the quantity and quality of the destruction and of the extent to which the recovery subsystem has been destroyed, meaning both changes in the composition and relations in the system, and changes in any possible subsystem that has recovery as a special task.

The destruction can be divided into destruction of human beings by killing and maiming them, destruction of human-made artefacts, destruction of society and destruction of nature. What are the recovery mechanisms, and how operational will they be?

As to killing: the recovery mechanism is *reproduction,* and it is generally feasible, otherwise humankind would not have reached its present size in spite of the many wars. The question, which is difficult to answer, is what will happen to human reproduction after a really massive onslaught, *viz.*

Will *demographic imbalances* slow down the recovery, women being somewhat more vulnerable than men so that the population pyramid may tilt in the opposite direction to what it usually does after a war?

Will a *lower propensity to reproduce,* partly because of the very harsh conditions into which offspring will be born, partly because of lack of faith in the long-term future given the evidence from the short-term past, slow down the recovery?

Will there be *dysgenic effects,* leading both to demographic imbalances and to a lower propensity to reproduce? – Will this be due to either negative selection of surviving parental stock or destruction of the genetic stock itself? Or will there be fears that this might be so?

As to maiming: health personnel in several countries have alerted the population (possibly also some politicians) to the destruction of the formal health sector[15] at the level of primary, secondary and tertiary health services – clinics, hospitals and homes. Even at their present level they are barely able to handle the regular health needs of the population, including accidents many orders of magnitude less destructive (in terms of wounded) than those predicted in a medium scenario in a war with weapons of mass destruction. The same would probably apply to the informal health sector. The capacity for self-care, mutual care and other care depends not only on the will, which may be questionable, but on the availability of, for instance, medicinal plants, fresh water, bandages. Folk medicine is by and large based on vulnerable, higher order plants, and even the simplest stocks of some curative medicine are likely to be depleted soon.

As to destruction of human-made artefacts: the recovery mechanism is *reconstruction.* Europe and Japan after the Second World War show that carpet-bombed cities exposed to firestorms have been reconstructed, even the two cities that were victims of nuclear bombs. However, at higher orders of magnitude of destruction two new phenomena, by no means unknown but increasingly important, will appear. First, reconstruction by own bootstraps seems unlikely after a destruction of such a deep scope over such an extensive domain. The resources may not only be unavailable locally, but also unavailable nationally, including the will to reconstruct as opposed to making do with survival in the ruins, scavenging and bartering, at a low level materially, probably also non-materially. Secondly the inputs for reconstruction have to come from the outside. But with the scope and domain of destruction envisaged here it is hard to see how recovery can be achieved without creating very deep and long-lasting dependency relations – much more so than the ties created in connection with the massive transfer from the USA to Europe known as Marshall Aid. In this case a relatively rich country had come out of the war unscathed. In a major nuclear war complete survival is likely only for relatively poor countries not themselves nuclear powers or satisfactory as nuclear theaters, and unable to undertake anything like a "massive transfer". This will change if sufficiently rich countries are saved, but then dependencies will result.

As to destruction of society: the recovery mechanism is *regeneration.* That some society in the broad sociological sense of the term will exist after massive destruction is not questioned, but this is not the same as regeneration to something similar to pre-attack society. It is a question of not only reconstructing the products (see above, the "artefacts") but of the production *capacity;* not only of distributing products but of building a distribution *mechanism;* not only of having *some* institutions, but *the* institutions one wants; not only of having *some* structure but *the* structure one wants; not only of having *some* culture but *the* culture that was cherished. Survival institutions, structures and cultures will always emerge, as in concentration-camps, in life-boats, among military, guerrillas and civilians during a battle, etc., but much more than that is wanted. The conditions for regenerating something similar to pre-attack society may simply not be present; it all depends on what kind of dialectic is set in motion by the onslaught. But whatever it is, the dialectic, as has been argued above, is unlikely to be of the type that will lead to societies that are better adapted to their environment than the present ones, or better adapted to human and social development.

As to destruction of nature: the recovery mechanism is called *renewal,* and it is not going to be easy, not even the simplified agricultural part. One possibility would be to start new types of agriculture with more complex patterns, poly-cultures, more imitative of mature eco-systems, reaping excess biomass produced from time to time for a number of purposes (e.g. combining agriculture, horticulture, aquaculture, with very high, not very low entropy). But it takes a long time to build productive, complex systems in a hostile environment.

Thus, the prospects are far from bright. And even military preparation, which is insignificant compared to military action, has some of
these effects and starts off some of the chains, cycles, and synergisms.
Many would actually argue that we are already living in maimed societies, waiting for the *coup de grâce*. But that might also, still, be too
pessimistic an interpretation.

3.4 Some scenarios

If instead of adding the tables we multiply them (as matrices, see the
appendix), we get the much more complex relations that have been
explored in the preceding pages. The consequences of one type of military activity are traced through the environmental, developmental and
military systems, in chains and cycles as long as one cares to make
them. The possibilities of this type of analysis have by no means been
exhausted; the above only indicates ways of thinking.

What emerges from this type of exercise is roughly speaking two
types of conclusions, both of them different ways of saying that we are
dealing with *systems* of elements, not only with *sets:*

(1) *The destructive effects are much more "widespread, longlasting
and severe" because of the chains, cycles and synergisms that are
operating.*

(2) *To undo the destruction is much more difficult because of the
changing composition of the sets and the destruction of recovery systems.*

Between these two factors there is also a synergism. The chains and
cycles will continue doing the destructive work particularly effectively
since no recovery is taking place. And because of this continued destruction, it will take particularly long for the composition to become
normal, and for the recovery systems to function adequately. Because
the environment is so destroyed development does not get off the
ground; because development does not start there will be no care for
the environment (the latter may also be true if there is maldevelopment in the sense of overdevelopment). Because social development is
so unsatisfactory human development does not take place. Because
maldeveloped (inconsiderate, combative, lacking solidarity) human
beings abound social development will not take place, and so on and
so forth.

The situation will be like Nevil Shute's *On the Beach* where environment is concerned, and like George Orwell's *1984* where development is concerned. It will be desertification, loneliness, and authoritarian societies at war, all in one.

Another way of summarizing the whole impact on environment-development would be to look at the extent of the destruction in space, time and spheres. Nuclear weapons in particular have three special characteristics in this regard:

Extension in space: by having the destructive agent, ionizing radiation, transported through space by wind in the atmosphere and by rivers, currents in the hydrosphere.

Extension in time: by using destructive agents with long-lasting destructive effect, radioactive elements with long half-lives, and with delayed effects such as cancer after a gestation period, possibly damage to genetic stock with transmission to offspring.[16]

Extension in sphere: by using the dependency chains among the spheres, with the homosphere depending on the biosphere and the biosphere on the other four, destruction in "lower" spheres will be transmitted to "higher" spheres.

This extension in sphere means that the destructive impact of nuclear weapons is not only higher for each sphere, but also more evenly distributed between spheres. This is the result of direct impact and goes via chains of the abiota → biota → abiota varieties. *In a sense these weapons are already environmental weapons,* even if they are not environmental modification weapons but "merely" make use of already existing cycles to obtain a multiplier effect. The extension in time is of a different nature, based on the deeper impact destruction can have when it affects the nuclei of atoms and genes, for instance with leukemia 6–9 years after exposure, cancer twenty years later or more.

This should be compared with warfare in earlier ages. Destruction was here and now and not so much there and afterwards; and it could, by and large, be limited to the homosphere – to humans and their settlements, possibly their agriculture. Any large-scale insult to the other spheres of the environment was out of question if for no other reason because technology was too "soft". Of course, incendiary weapons, high explosives, chemical, biological and radiological weapons may all tend in the direction of extension when used on a massive scale. Only nuclear arms will *always* lead to extension.

Most scenarios trying to come to grips with what a world after a major nuclear exchange would look like commit one simple methodological mistake. They describe only the destroyed part and the extent of the destruction, not its relation to a possible nondestroyed part. And this is not necessarily because they assume all of the world to be equally destroyed, for that would imply a symmetry in the destruction totally out of touch with both political/military and physical reality – granting that atmosphere and hydrosphere currents will have a certain distributive effect. Rather, they simply forget the other part, or find it irrelevant, *or too painful to consider*.

But it is not irrelevant. How is a basically intact region likely to behave relative to a large and basically destroyed region, in the same country, continent or world in general? With a destruction involving fundamental degradation of the environment, killing and maiming millions and destroying social fabric and artefacts? While the survivors may be carriers of diseases and radionuclides? Answer: *in all likelihood by quarantining them*. An intact local, national, regional or world government can perhaps force a devastated population through evacuation on a "host community" (or country or region). But we have no world or regional governments with such powers, and the national government in the destroyed country is likely to function well below its usual level. Much more likely is a process of brutalization adding to the other processes, simply keeping the victims away, by force, on the other side of the fence/border. And the same will probably happen inside that fence: killing those who are too ill, in addition to the old and crippled and insane – everybody who consumes without producing – perhaps under the pretext of euthanasia.[17] Outsiders may control all such processes through *occupation*.

But the processes will be reinforced by the mirror feeling among the surviving victims: a guilt, both towards the dead, for having survived and towards the non-hit, for having been hit, like the Japanese *hibakusha*.[18] What right do I have to survive? And at the same time "I am hit, I am no longer normal, I am a carrier of the latter-day leprosy, I will be a burden out of proportion to anything I can offer". Thinking of the medical expenses in connection with, for instance, peacetime cancer treatment, this perception is no doubt correct. In short: they may to a large extent submit to the quarantine.

Will a heavily asymmetric distribution of the victims lead to very different domestic and global structures? Not necessarily: numerical preponderance is not the same as power over social structures and other resources. But it helps. It stands to reason that the point of gravity, at least for some time, in global relations will move towards the South, the Third (and Fourth) World – and away from the major belligerents in a major First World–Second World conflagration. Similar remarks can be made about the intrasocietal translation of new distributions into new structures, although the reasoning here is more theoretical than empirical.[19]

And this opens for a new dimension to the analysis. It is the threat not of being extinguished, nor that others will be permitted to continue living, *but that others may even take over, be in command,* and *may even do better.* In other words not only will the belligerents not be missed, their premature departure through self-destruction (thinking now of the North) may even be seen as a blessing in disguise. The vision of a Northern space, comprising all major industrial/urban sites in North America, Europe and the Soviet Union destroyed and incapable of regenerating themselves is too horrible for the North to contemplate. Does it help to know that when the radiation has reached an acceptable level the South may move in and put it under administration as a protectorate incapable of self-government, possibly helped by Chinese labor, Japanese capital/technology, Swiss banks and Red Cross, if these three countries have managed to come through relatively unscathed?[20] *Or does it make it worse?* And if it does – could that be one factor stemming the tide towards omnicide?

4. Security:
The overarching concept

4.1. The concept of security

Security is the probability that a system can be sustained – a human system, a social system or a world system.

The focus in the following will be on *social* systems or societies, "countries" as they are commonly conceived of. The security of the *human* system is usually referred to as *health* and can be seen as a positive balance between the resistance capacity of the human body and the level of exposure to destructive health hazards of various kinds. Life is an internal dialectic between the two ending with death. Preventive medicine (primary and secondary prophylaxis) and the capacity for repair when damage is wrought, curative medicine (primary, secondary and tertiary health care) are nevertheless highly meaningful, postponing death. The security of the *world* system is not so much explored as unthreatened; there are no credible external threats to the world as a whole at present, but it is sometimes referred to in terms of "survival probabilities for the human species". But the focus here is on social security, of countries. A "security doctrine" is a theory of this security.

"Sustaining a society" can mean a combination of two things:

(1) that the society remains essentially stable, *and*

(2) that any basic change is essentially from the inside (endogenous); brought about by the internal dialectic of the society

In liberal thinking this "internal dialectic" would have to be by democratic processes such as voting (in assemblies and/or the population). In marxist thinking it would be by letting the *internal* contradictions work themselves out so that history, even History, can run its course. But there is basic agreement that the change should not be imposed from the outside; outside intervention being a fundamentally marxist act.

75

The question, then, is not *whether* security is desirable. There is a broad consensus about this as evidenced by the many references to "self-determination", "non-interference in internal affairs" and their equivalents. The question is *how* to obtain security. The question is important because security is the basic rationale of the military system, held by many to be not only necessary but also sufficient. But military systems are also a threat, both to environment and development, as indicated above. Is there a way out of this dilemma?

4.2. Conventional security doctrines

Conventional doctrine rests on the assumption that only a (strong) military system can effectively deter force (attacks) and threats of force (blackmail) aiming at changing the society, and also provide the means of fighting if the attack is not deterred. The exploration below does not actually challenge these two assumptions in the military doctrine but modifies them and embeds them in what is seen here as a more comprehensive and also more realistic doctrine of security.

On what does security, as defined above, depend? One would believe, to use the parallel from health above, that it would have something to do with the level of "resistance" to destruction of a given society and its capacity to detain, reduce, fight the "exposure" from the outside. The terms that can be used in an analysis of health, however, are not necessarily the most felicitous in an analysis of security. Instead of "resistance" one might prefer "invulnerability" ("robustness" is another possibility). And instead of "exposure" one might say "destruction". Thus, the security of an armoured knight with a lance facing another of the same type has to do with the strength of his armour, the capacity for destruction of the other side and the knight's ability to destroy that capacity. In a formula: $I_1-(D_2-D_1(D_2))$, where I_1 is the level of invulnerability of Party$_1$, D_2 the destructive capability of Party$_2$ and D_1 (D_2) the ability of Party$_1$ to destroy this destructive capacity. It is invulnerability minus *net* destruction.

The formula can also be written:

Security = Invulnerability + defensive capability
            – outside offensive capability

Since what the outside does can only be influenced, not controlled, by oneself this indicates two ways of increasing one's own security: increasing the invulnerability level of one's own society, *and* increasing the defensive capability (the capacity to reduce outside destructive capability). So the knight is safe if his armour is strong enough to withstand the *net* impact that reaches him.

But this is only a first approximation formula, with which most people would probably agree. The question is how one implements it, in very concrete terms. Exactly what do we mean by invulnerability, and what do we mean by defensive capability? It is only by being spelled out that the statement can become non-trivial. But the moment it is spelled out it also becomes politically controversial, partly because of the vested interests involved, since different answers may give power and privilege to different groups, and partly because there are so many answers and no generally agreed-upon method, so far, for selecting the best answer or class of answers.

However, before we proceed with one possible list of answers, let us look at the matter from the other party's point of view, the one with the "outside offensive capability". Why should he want to use force, or threat of force? He must have not only a capability, but also a motivation. There is something he wants in or from the society of Party$_1$. That "something" can conveniently be divided into economic, political, military, social and cultural values. To wit:

Economic values: access to raw materials and to markets; generally making the country a part of the external sector of the economy

Political values: to obtain general support, e.g. in the UN and IGOs; generally making the country a political ally

Military values: securing strategic positions and raw materials and denying them to the other side; buffer zone; generally making the country a military ally; show prowess

Social values: reproducing oneself in the social formation of another country, thereby extending oneself

Cultural values: inculcating one's own (deep) culture in others; missionary zeal, confirming one's own culture

It is naive to believe that countries act aggressively, using force or threats of force, only out of economic motivation. Of course, it may be argued that political and military aggression ultimately serve economic goals. But they may also serve social and cultural goals, e.g. the missionary compulsion to spread one's own cultural values and social institutions around the world. And military aggression may also be a goal in its own right.

Conventional doctrine holds that the propensity to use or threaten to use that "outside offensive capability" is proportionate to the balance in a cost benefit analysis: the value of what one can obtain *minus* the costs of attaining it, meaning the destruction of value and force wrought upon oneself by the party attacked. If the value is V, then the motivation should be proportionate to

$$Motivation = K(V - (D_1 - D_2 (D_1) - I_2) - D_1 (D_2))$$

It should be remembered that the counter-value destruction wrought on Party$_2$ is the negative of its security – that is the first term in what has to be subtracted from the value gained; in addition there is the counter-force destruction of the destructive capability of Party$_2$. This can also be written in this way:

Motivation has to do with:
    Value hoped for + own invulnerability
    − outside offensive capability to destroy
    + how much one hopes to destroy of that
    − how much the other side can destroy of one's own capacity to
      destroy

Now back to Party$_1$ again. Party$_1$ is not only interested in defending itself in case of attack; it is above all interested in preventing the attack completely. In other words, Party$_1$ wants Party$_2$ to come to the decision that "attack does not pay", and refrain from the attack. From the formula above there are five possibilities; three factors should be decreased and two should be increased to be on the safe side. This can be simplified into two not mutually exclusive approaches: to decrease the gains, and/or to increase the costs to the attacker.

There are many ways of doing the former. One would be to get rid of the valued assets before the other side gets hold of them, e.g. by depleting the stocks (say, of oil) as quickly as possible; by fighting so that the other side itself destroys what it covets (through trip-wire mechanisms); or through scorched-earth tactics. Another would be to be "negatively even-handed," denying the value not only to one side but also to the other. In practice this would mean to deny such military values as establishing bases or even to become a satellite, not only to one party but to all parties, through non-alignment. A third one would be to be "positively even-handed" – giving something to both sides.

However, there will always be certain values that are coveted and not to be conceded under any conditions, like basic decision-making. Many of them are in the field of social and cultural values and can be translated into questions of freedom (from social repression) and identity (with own culture) – in other words in terms of nonmaterial needs. The fact is that people are often more willing to put up a fight for these nonmaterial needs than for some gains in material standard of living – and even willing to sacrifice the most basic material value of them all – their own lives, their bodily survival – in the struggle.

From this point on it is impossible to continue any discussion without a key distinction between two types of destructive agents or action: *defensive* and *offensive*. The obvious circumstance that there is a grey zone in between should not serve as an excuse to disregard this distinction between means of destruction that are *stationary or mobile with a short range* and hence non-provocative, and those that are *mobile with a range sufficient to have a destructive impact outside one's country*, on second and third parties. These are objective aspects of a weapons system, although capable of transformation towards the more offensive or the more defensive. At any given time the maximum range of a weapons system is an objective fact and this is what analysis should focus on, not on the declarations accompanying research and development, production and deployment, etc, of a system.[1] A weapons system that *can* be used for offense *is* offensive; one that cannot be so used is defensive. A mixture of the two is offensive. And what is offensive is provocative regardless of intentions.

The cost-benefit analysis of whether to build one's security mainly on defensive or mainly on offensive weapons is complex and depends on many factors. If the purpose is to increase the costs to the other side of an attack (not only decreasing the gains), then there can be no doubt that an offensive counter-attack can destroy much more of the other side than a defensive counter-attack. The former is against the whole of the other side, force *and* value; the latter only against the little he sends into one's own territory, in other words mainly "force", and not all of that. Reflections such as these lead some countries to develop highly offensive capabilities, as is well known.

However, there is the problem that the other side may do the same or prepare for it, and the net result is a race in offensive arms capability, another well-known aspect of the world today. The offensive capability is divided, not sharply, into a counter-value capability (high yield, high or low precision) and a counter-force capability (high or low yield, high precision) – meaning that with increasing precision there *may* be a transition from counter-value towards counter-force strategy, from destroying the other party to destroying his ability to destroy oneself. Both enter the formula above as D°_1 or D°_2 (the superscript stands for offensive) and $D^\circ_1(D^\circ_2)$ or $D^\circ_2(D^\circ_1)$ respectively. $D^\circ_1-D^\circ_2(D^\circ_1)$ and $D^\circ_2-D^\circ_1(D^\circ_2)$ are what is left for a second strike after a counter-force first strike has taken its toll; the problem is whether it is sufficient to produce "unacceptable damage". And this is a question of balance between destructive yield and invulnerability level, the invulnerability of force in a counter-force attack (e.g. hardening) and the invulnerability of value in a counter-value attack (e.g. civil defense). The formulas for all of this can be written out. They become somewhat longer but the logic is always the same: destructive capacity, invulnerability of that which is to be destroyed; destruction of the destructive capacity and invulnerability of the destructive capacity. And this actually opens up four different aspects of the arms race: ability to destroy value, ability to destroy force, invulnerability of value, invulnerability of force. Four different components of the arms race, all of them important.

It goes almost without saying that a race as complex as this will not become stable. There is no stable equilibrium point. There are too many variables, too many uncertainties, too many difficult comparisons between noncommensurate, even incongruous entities to be made. And it is not only a question of four more or less parallel components of the arms race; each component has itself several sub-components. There are *types* of destructive agent, *types* of invulnerability. The result is the monstrous arsenal of highly destructive offensive weapons we have and the prospects of very basic destruction if they are unleashed. Hence it is not strange that disarmament negotiations lead nowhere. Efforts to outlaw the invulnerability approach (Anti-ABM treaty)[2] are almost schizophrenic, and stimulate the offensive race further.

There are actually three separate problems in connection with these offensive arms:

(1) they cannot be used to ensure security because the destruction level of even a second strike is too high. No invulnerability can compensate adequately, military action will destroy what military preparation is supposed to protect.

(2) they cannot be used to obtain political (or other) goals either; they will destroy what they are supposed to deliver – unless they are used for blackmail and that is only possible if one side has absolute superiority. They are the end to politics rather than the continuation of politics with other means.

(3) they lead to arms races that get out of hand, both in the sense that no stable point can be found, and in the sense that with increasingly complex systems there is an increasing probability that preparation will be translated into action, i.e. war.

All of this has also been to some extent true of conventional offensive weapons. But today it is true at a level of destructiveness unheard of in earlier epochs – as elaborated in the preceding chapters. In short: *this is no longer a doctrine of security. It is irrationality.*[3]

The question, then, is *whether a doctrine of security can be based on invulnerability and defensive capability rather than the mutually assured destruction of very high levels of offensive capability* (see the formula for security). In practice it will always be based on all three, but it is a question of changing the point of gravity towards the first two rather than the last one. One rationale for this would be what has already been mentioned: although an arms race between entirely defensive weapons is not inconceivable, however irrational, a race between defensive systems on one side and offensive systems on the other is very possible, and a race between offensive systems is almost a tautology. But there is also another reason which has to do with an internal linkage between the level of invulnerability and the defensive/offensive distinction: *the more vulnerable the society, the higher the probability that it will have offensive weapons systems,* for a variety of reasons. To explore this the invulnerability dimensions have to be spelled out, and this will be done in the next section.

It can be objected that with more precise weapons than those we have today the yield can be lower and hence there will be less destruction – except of the precise target. The weapons could then again be used for security purposes in a more precise, political sense. But there are at least three considerations:

(1) The number of bombs must be increased because of the obvious counter-strategy of scattering the force to be hit and of increasing the number of weapons.

(2) Force is often located so close to value that a neat geographical separation between counter-force and counter-value strategies becomes impossible.

(3) Nor is a neat strategic separation possible: there is no basis for assuming that a war will be either counter-force or counter-value. The party with more precise weapons may prefer the former; the party with less precise weapons will answer with the latter – including launching counter-value weapons in the warning that counter-force weapons are on the way.[4]

What is true is that increasing precision complicates the scenarios for a possible nuclear war. And one may ask the question: what happens when the precision becomes so high (CEP down to some dozens or scores of meters) that conventional weapons could do the job? If it is a question of merely destroying a missile on the other side, would not classical sabotage be a far simpler and also less devastating approach for both sides? Are not the weapons of mass destruction, in fact, non-weapons, and is that not an argument for a return to conventional arms?

However that may be, the *basic* weakness of conventional security doctrine can perhaps now be stated. Both parties pursue offensive capacity and the ability to destroy that offensive capacity. *But there is no balance point.* At the end of this process there is only more of the same process. If there had been a well-defined point where both parties could say "Here we are, this is it," then that point might offer security. The absence of such a point is perhaps the key argument against the whole approach. It is impossible as far as one can see to stabilize the system. Additional ability to destroy value or force, or ability to make value or force less vulnerable only lead to new races, and hence not to more security. Of a security doctrine one should demand that it sets in motion a process that increases rather than decreases security, and one should demand a balance point. Conventional doctrines do not seem to pass that test.

4.3. Alternative security doctrines

There are many aspects of *invulnerability,* and there is much that analysts of social systems can learn from the analysis of eco-systems. More particularly, the notion of maturity of an eco-system, based on diversity and symbiosis, as a key to resilience, is useful, although it should be applied with care: There is more to human social systems than to eco-systems. Invulnerability will be discussed at five levels (or "spaces"): inter-national, national, intra-national or social, local, and individual.

At the *inter-national (global or humankind) level,* invulnerability is best promoted by making the world *a global and stable eco-system,* with diversity (pluralism) among the components (countries, nations) and symbiosis, meaning exchange for mutual benefit. This symbiosis, however, has to be equitable (not only "mutual"), which it is usually not in nature. Humans are perfectly capable of highly predatory types of symbiosis, as between colony and colonizer. But it is also the hallmark of humans that they are capable of creating structures of equitable symbiosis. "Diversity combined with equitable symbiosis" is another ecological way of expressing the idea of "active peaceful co-existence between different systems". "Stable eco-system" is another way of warning against environmental deterioration. But to this should also be added global selfrepair institutions of all kinds to undo damage – the global parallel to cure by the body itself – by such organizations as the Red Cross, UNDRO, UNICEF, UNEP, WHO. In one formula: in such a world invulnerability would be promoted by countries being mutually useful to each other, and for that to happen the countries have to be diverse (not merely reproductions of each other) and relate symbiotically and equitably to each other. If one of the models for making societies proves to be maladaptive, diversity guarantees that there are other models.

At the *national level* invulnerability is best promoted by making the *country come closer to a stable eco-system.* From an environmental point of view this means adequate control of pollution, depletion and maturity (watching the relative frequency of biota and abiota). It would also argue against highly unstable, dangerous systems like nuclear power plants, waste disposal, etc. From an economic point of view this means a relatively high level of national *self-sufficiency,* in

83

other words not relying on outside eco-systems by depleting them, possibly also polluting them and reducing their maturity. But at the same time the hypothesis in the preceding paragraph was that there ought to be symbiosis, even equitable, between nations/countries. It is precisely this apparent contradiction between national self-sufficiency and international interdependence that the concept of *self-reliance* aims at resolving, *combining self-sufficiency in essentials with equitable exchange of other goods/services:* Essentials would be everything that is needed for the satisfaction of the most basic needs of the population: food, health inputs, energy and weapons. To this list could be added clothes/shelter, schools and some others, but they are not so quickly depleted, and hence there is less necessity for an uninterrupted flow of inputs. If these are not produced inside the country it will be easily blackmailed into surrender or subjugation by those who use food as a weapon, health as a weapon, energy as a weapon and/or weapons as a weapon, by controlling the inputs into the country. But beyond this level of essentials the field is open for exchange, using the world market to ensure symbiosis and world planning to ensure equity – the market certainly does not guarantee that. As there are security benefits both from independence and interdependence (but not from dependence) one should bet on both. Self-reliance does precisely that.

At the *intra-national or social level* much the same argument applies as for the international level. The parts – districts, organizations, associations – have to relate to each other symbiotically and equitably to tie the system together. They should be diverse in order to provide the resilience that makes a system less vulnerable. If everything is done in the same way (all factories organized the same way, all hospitals and schools, all districts) then whatever is wrong with one of them would apply to the whole system. A system that walks on two or more legs will always have something to fall back upon. Equity without diversity only leads to a highly vulnerable homogeneity. But diversity without equity is no good either. Separate, apart(heid), and particularly when in addition exploited, does not become equal. Such societies are riddled with cleavages between classes, ethnic and racial groups, sex and age groups, districts, and each cleavage reduces the invulnerability by reducing the motivation of the dominated to defend the system, as well as the possibility that the other side may make use of the cleavage for their own purposes. Hence, *intra-national invulnerability is above all promoted by overcoming cleavages caused by injustice, inequality and inequity,* weaving the social system together, if not seamlessly, at least without ridges.

At the *local level* much the same argument applies as at the national level. Invulnerability is best promoted by making the *local level, district, come closer to a stable eco-system.* From an environmental point of view this means adequate control of *local* pollution, depletion and maturity. This, in turn, means that as many eco-cycles ("eco" actually standing both for ecological and economic) as possible should be within the local community, i.e. using local raw materials for local production for local consumption. For it is only at the local level that eco-cycles can become sufficiently transparent to people in general, making both producers and consumers aware of the implications of depletion, pollution and decreasing maturity. It is at the local level that people can suffer the consequences of their own maladaptive behavior, and cut down on the feedback lag so that control is possible – particularly if all kinds of voluntary organizations help with this endeavour.

This means, economically speaking, a higher level of local self-reliance, again meaning self-sufficiency in staples and equitable exchange beyond that. Needless to say, given the asymmetry of economic geography, this is not always possible so it should be seen as a goal to be approximated and to be prepared for. For this to happen administrative borders at the local level, between municipalities, are not necessarily the best guide. Ideally the borders should be drawn so as to make local self-reliance more possible, around key eco-cycles for the production of essentials.

At the *individual level* invulnerability is probably best promoted by having individuals with a *way of life that is satisfactory.* If it is highly unsatisfactory, if people are starved (including sexual frustration), repressed, one may get a population excellently suited to attack, for *offense* in order to obtain satisfaction – a method used by authoritarian regimes. But if people good for *defense* are wanted, a satisfactory way of life is better. This should not be confused merely with a higher material standard of living. When there are doubts today about the invulnerability of the (Western) societies with the highest material standard of living, and there is a feeling that the population has become "soft", then this may also be because the population is *not* satisfied with such a way of life. So much of the social structure drives social action in a materialistic direction, making people believe that they want ever more growth in material things. People then get confused because satisfaction does not follow. In that confusion a basic source of vulnerability can probably be located. A satisfactory way of life, it seems, is also based on the pillars of diversity and symbiosis. People in modern society live long lives, and probably need to have a diversity of experience through their life cycle for life not to become oppressive, however materially enriching it is. But these phases in the life-cycle should relate symbiotically, one phase contributing to the next. Ideally there should be both a feeling of many lives to be lived and a feeling of having lived a complete life when the end is near. A good society is one that provides both. And in that society that intangible quality, *a high morale,* should emerge.

As the reader can verify, these five spaces or aspects of invulnerability are compatible with each other, but incompatible with many structures found in the world of today. To mention just two examples: they presuppose a high level of individual, local and national autonomy in decision-making, meaning a high level of decentralization. But how can this be combined with all the coordination needed for symbiosis and equity? At this point what self-reliance is for the economy in terms of resolving contradictions *federalism* is for the polity. At the international level this is to a large extent what the United Nations system is trying to do. The problem is found at the lower levels. And this is the second example: if the local level is dependent on a technology supplied and administered by the national level, which in turn depends on a technology supplied and administered by some other country, then both levels are vulnerable, and even more so if the technology itself is vulnerable. This is even more true of military technology; dependency on superpowers tends to lead to demobilization of national defense; dependency on the center to demobilization at local level.

So far the reasoning has been from the outside in: what would make a society least vulnerable to attack? But one could also, and should, reason the other way, from the inside out: what kind of society is most likely to engage in attack? The vulnerable or the invulnerable? In short, what is the relation between the two key variables in this analysis, invulnerable/vulnerable and offensive/defensive? Which society is more, which is less dangerous to its environment?

The Table contains our hypotheses:

Table 7. *Level of danger **to others***
        as a function of vulnerability and weapons system

	Offensive weapons systems	Defensive weapons systems
Socio-economically invulnerable societies	MOST DANGEROUS	LEAST DANGEROUS
Socio-economically vulnerable societies	SECOND MOST DANGEROUS	THIRD MOST DANGEROUS

That the combination of invulnerability and offensive systems is dangerous is obvious. This is the system that has a secured base and can launch its attack unpunished. This is why massive civil defense programs in superpowers are so frightening.[5] But a vulnerable society with offensive weapons is also very dangerous. The basic hypothesis is thus that *the more vulnerable the society, the more it will tend to acquire offensive weapons systems, and possibly engage in offensive politics.* The reasons for this are connected with the five levels of reasoning above, and will be spelled out below.

At the *international level:* the society becomes aggressive when it fails to respect the rules of a global, stable eco-system. Alone or to-gether with others it may share major responsibility for environmental deterioration at the global level, thus increasing the gaps between the demands on the global eco-system and what that system can produce without further deterioration. It may also fail to respect the rule of equity, not only symbiosis – getting into endless actio-reactio chains between those who want to liberate themselves from exploitation, and those who want to maintain the inequities. To maintain the status quo it becomes offensive, fighting wars far away from home.

At the *national level:* the society becomes aggressive when it moves further away from a national, stable eco-system and has depleted the stock and polluted so much that it has to go abroad to secure even the staples.[6] A self-sufficient country does not have to do that, and a self-reliant one at least does not have to do it for essentials. Abroad it will increasingly find countries in the same predicament, not – as was held to be the case before – countries with such an underconsumption of what their eco-systems produced that it was only fair and beneficial to both to make eco-cycles that connect over-consumers and under-consumers (relative to their eco-system basis). The "law" of comparative advantages gave the economistic rationale for this pattern. But today the level of consciousness is much higher all around the world so this behavior easily translates into open conflict, with the country that misuses someone else's eco-system increasingly seen as the aggressor. With increasing industrialization everybody is pressing their eco-system to the limit, and then turning to the points of least resistance on the outside.

At the *intra-national level:* the society may become aggressive, as the adage has it, in order to direct attention away from internal cleavages, using conflict without to conceal conflict within. In addition to this, the more vulnerable the society is, the more easily it can be destroyed, for instance by destroying an administrative center, a corporate center, or a center in the technosphere. And the less it can afford to have the war on its own ground, preferring to export it through the use of offensive weapons systems with long-distance weapons carriers.

At the *local level:* following up what has just been said, if the local level does not possess a minimum autonomy, if there is no local self-reliance and no stability in the local eco-system, then the local level becomes dependent on the center and unable to launch its own defense. A spirit of capitulation will easily set in when the center no longer works. The center, knowing this, will be even more inclined to resort to offensive weapons. And if the other side is steered by the same logic they will fight the war in the middle, on the territory of a third party.

At the *individual level:* the less satisfactory the life style (and this is to a large extent a question of how the society has managed to stabilize the whole eco-system with the humans in it), the more frustrated and hence aggressive the population. One case is unemployment. As it rises the basis for a policy of aggression becomes more solid. And unemployment, in turn, may have its roots in overproduction, relative to effective demand for the products. One reason for this may be too high a level of productivity to employ a sufficient number of people productively. Another may be too great a dependence on external markets for demand. And external markets may be penetrated by other suppliers and/or be supplied by internal production. In either case one may say that ecological principles have not been respected: there is an overutilization of the productive capacity of some components in the system, with very high productivity, and there is an over-extension of eco-cycles, through too much trade, to the point where they become very vulnerable.

The position argued is not national or even local autarchy. The idea has been that invulnerability is served by combining a high level of stability of the eco-system at national and local levels with symbiotic linkages at the international and "interlocal" (i.e. intranational) levels. In other words, by striving towards self-sufficiency nationally/locally in staples, and exchange beyond that. The concept of "self-reliance", as mentioned, is intended to serve exactly this purpose. It should be pointed out that the self-sufficiency part does not even have to be operational in normal periods as long as there are provisions for making it operational in times of crisis – with stocks to fill the gap between dependency on the outside and autonomous production in a transition period.

So far the point has been made that invulnerability is intrinsically tied to environmental principles, not only in the sense that the stability of the eco-system enters as a key necessary condition, but also in the sense that there is much to learn from the built-in wisdom of a mature eco-system. According to the above reasoning, vulnerable societies will tend to develop offensive weapons systems, (1) because they have to export the battle-field since their own system is too brittle to stand the impact of a war, (2) because they need offensive weapons to carry out the aggressive acts to balance the eco-system in their own favor by extending it, e.g. to secure key raw materials to make up for deficits due to depletion at home. The invulnerable system, it is argued, can better afford a defensive weapons system because the two conditions above do not obtain, or obtain much less. But what, then, would a defensive defense system look like?

Again, ecological reasoning may be helpful. A defense system should, in order not to be too vulnerable, itself be highly diverse, develop a high level of symbiosis among the components, and satisfy the principles of national and local autonomy indicated above. A defense system based on a narrow band of destruction and value-denial capability (e.g. only conventional military), and highly centralized in the sense that the local units depend on national decision-making, and the national units on international decision-making (through alliance systems), may look very strong, but has important vulnerabilities built into it. Thus, a conflict may develop in such a way that a narrow military capability becomes less relevant or irrelevant, like strategic nuclear arms against guerrillas. Destruction or internal collapse of international decision-making may leave the national systems confused and indecisive since centralization always implies a certain demobilization of the periphery. And the local/national level will not only depend on national/international decisions, but also on supply of hardware inputs with technologies that are increasingly complex the more removed they are from the local level.

Just as the above reasoning was in terms of eco-cycles, one might reason in terms of *defense cycles* with software and hardware inputs and outputs in terms of destruction – with the side effects of depletion (of raw materials, capital, ultimately of arms and soldiers) and pollution (e.g. material remnants of war), and degradation of the whole environment in general terms. For the cycle not to be too vulnerable it should not be too extended or too dependent on outside inputs. Ideally *the defense cycle should be stable.* And this, in ecological language, is the key point in the theory of guerrilla warfare. The fish in the water should not pollute the water on which it depends for supply, including the supply of people who take the place of those who are incapacitated through the fighting (killed and wounded).

In concrete terms this means that a defensive defense system, in addition to the characteristic given it by definition, of being unsuited for offensive attack, should operate in units that are *small, dispersed, mobile, autonomous* and *supported locally.* As ground rules for guerrilla fighting this today is a part of world culture, reinforced by the remarkable success of this type of military system against over-powerful military systems that are also mobile, across borders, even continents, but big, concentrated, centralized and based far away. The latter may have a very much higher destructive yield, but is essentially useless. First, there is the fear of retaliation when nuclear power is no longer a monopoly. Second, nuclear power against a paramilitary force that is small, dispersed, mobile, etc. has as its consequence total, omnicidal destruction – i.e. no longer politics.

These rules apply not only to effective fighting, basing as they do the defense cycles locally so that support is less easily exhausted and the destructive impact less great and more dispersed than it is with weapons of mass destruction on both sides. They are also principles for increasing the invulnerability of one's own means of destruction. They should never be concentrated so that they can be destroyed by one well-directed, devastating attack, e.g. with nuclear arms. As such the rules would apply not only to paramilitary components of a total defense concept, but to conventional military and nonmilitary (civilian resistance) components as well. Among these three components there could be a symbiotic division of labor, e.g. with the conventional military given more first-line defense tasks (but not necessarily at the perimeter of the national land, water and air space), with "smart" rockets, fortifications, etc. to counter invading forces;[7] and the other two, paramilitary and nonmilitary, more in-depth defense tasks – territorial defense and social defense, respectively. A capitulation concept would only apply to the conventional military defense, and might even be ruled out for the other two.

In principle a defense such as this could have both a high deterrence effect by making the country look highly "indigestible" precisely because there is no way of destroying the defense by attacking a limited number of key points. Its invulnerability lies in a double resilience. If defense is given up in one part of the national territory it can still continue in another because of the high level of autonomy, and if one type of defense is given up (e.g. conventional) it can still continue with other types. The system is, like any system, vulnerable to threats of total destruction through a counter-value or even counter-force nuclear attack. But that vulnerability also exists with any other type of defense system. We live in an age where absolute defense is no longer possible because absolute destruction is possible. A "mini-nuke" smuggled into a country, placed in a locker and equipped with an electronic ignition device is already such a weapon.

In principle this should also be the type of defense that is less destructive if it is really in the hands of the defenders themselves. Being rooted locally there would be a vested interest in minimizing the destruction of people, material and environment. A centralized national army might be less considerate of the local community, even easily sacrifice it "in the national interest". Correspondingly the international army may sacrifice a whole society in the interest of the collective security. The pollution of the environment through the material remnants of war is more easily done in far-away places.[8] Thus, the localized defense cycle mobilizes some of the same mechanisms as the localized eco-cycle: the negative effects are more obvious and more important because those who live there have to suffer the consequences themselves. In addition the feedback lag is cut down because the distance between destructive agent and victim is shorter. There is no illusion that a war would not be very destructive; this is only an effort to point to some factors that might reduce the destructiveness and at the same time provide a good basis for a defense. At the same time it is indicated that there is a certain compatibility between this way of defending oneself and the various ways of obtaining a higher level of invulnerability. The key link is contraction, diversification and solidification of the various cycles on which human society is based, but not to the point that equitable exchanges at the international and national levels are neglected.

Why do we have so many defense systems in the world that are offensive rather than defensive, granting again the vast, intermediate grey zone between the defensive and the offensive? Partly because so many societies are so vulnerable, and becoming even more so. Also because they grew out of a tradition of offensive rather than defensive purposes, bridged by the adage that "offense is the best defense". The old ministries of war have only recently become ministries of defense – without necessarily undergoing any transformation other than semantic. An offensive capacity has to become not only highly mobile and long range, but also big, concentrated (over a broad front, though), centralized and of course not supported locally since it is directed against any given level on the other side. This aggressive structure, then, sticks, and in an era where the defensive function is supposed to be the only legitimate one, strategies have to be found whereby essentially offensive military structures can be made at least to appear compatible with defensive functions. In addition any defense system presupposes an outside threat image. If the strategy is offensive the image has to be even more massive in order to justify the enormous destruction envisaged. Experience seems to indicate that for the other side it will be very difficult not to do the same. It will also develop offensive capacity and highly "offensive" (in the double sense of that term) and alienating images of the other side. The image justifies the arms, the arms have to be justified by the images, and an image–arms cycle is started that injects psychological fuel into the arms–arms cycles at the level of offensive arms because offensive arms are so provocative, so threatening. The result is the run-away race we know.

Between these two socio-economic and defense formations, one based on vulnerable eco-systems (both ecologically and economically) and on offensive weapons systems, and the other on more stable eco-systems and defensive weapons systems, there is a considerable distance. There are several dimensions to this type of process and many rungs on the ladders, steps on the road. *Thinking about the truly unthinkable* (which is not the implications of a war with weapons of mass destruction – that had been thought and rethought very many times even before Hiroshima), viz. *the whole problématique of alternative security doctrines more suited to our fragile world* is not served by absolutist approaches to difficult but necessary transitions. The call for "total transformation here and now" is counterproductive because it is impossible – the structures supporting the vulnerable/offensive combination, e.g. the entire world trade structure and the inner construction of most nation states, being too solid, too deeply entrenched. For this reason some efforts have been made above to indicate some of the sub-dimensions beneath the over-arching two: invulnerability, and defensive weapons systems.

A transformation process, then, could be slow or quick. Several countries, even in Europe, are very far advanced into what is here seen as the more positive combination,[9] others lag far behind. But in addition to the *speed* of any transformation process there is also the problem of how *parallel* the processes are. Imagine a country that increases its invulnerability but keeps its offensive system unchanged. It has been argued above that this would be an even more dangerous combination because the country might be able to get away with a major offensive attack relatively unpunished, which is the reason why the superpowers have agreed to remain to some extent vulnerable in the sense that their offensive systems should have a certain vulnerability built into them – the anti-ABM treaty.

Correspondingly, imagine the opposite process: the defense system is changed from predominantly offensive to predominantly defensive but the vulnerability level is left unchanged. The system certainly becomes less dangerous to others since it cannot launch an attack, but also more dangerous to itself because of its vulnerability. Moreover, there is something unstable in a combination that encourages the belief that the country might easily return to offensive systems, and since such a return cannot be developed overnight it would probably be through alliance formation. This points to the possible interest superpowers may have in encouraging the vulnerability of others so that they can become military clients, located on the periphery of defense cycles controlled by the superpowers themselves.

But in spite of such obvious constraints on the transformation process it is hard to believe that there will be no such process. The present system is simply so grossly maladapted[10] to its tasks and to the nature of the world as an eco-system that there must be some limit to its survival capacity. Maybe a parallel can be drawn here that cautions against any excessive optimism, yet opens for some: tobacco smoking, a highly maladaptive pattern of behavior. It is well known that faced with the evidence many people stop smoking whereas others continue or start. They may not know the evidence, may know it but not believe it, may believe it but not pay attention to it. One reason for the latter is, of course, that smoking serves a number of personal and social functions, both as a stimulant and as a tranquilizer, as entertainment, as a social act of belongingness to adult society, to a group, etc. Antismoking campaigns would probably be most successful if (1) they point out the danger of smoking, (2) point out what functions smoking serves, (3) do not necessarily reject these functions but even accept them and (4) indicate acceptable alternatives for all of them, although possibly not for all them in one stroke. Many smokers give up giving up simply because their restless search for alternatives is so unsuccessful and often unaided. It is easier for the resourceful – First World men, middle-aged, educated – to stop smoking: they may have many more alternatives than Third World young women.

Correspondingly it may be felt that we would make more progress today if at least as much energy were put into developing alternative security doctrines as into attacking the doctrines we have. This is a key point at which both the ecology and the peace movements in a sense have failed. Ecologists have not explored sufficiently the war/peace aspects of environmental politics, in spite of the obvious fact that there is no greater threat to the environment than a major modern war. And the peace movement has not explored sufficiently the ecological aspects of the whole war/peace issue, in spite of the fact that wars are so often over scarce resources, and also have the environment as a target. Both of them have taken developmental aspects of their concerns into account, however. What has been missing is the triangular concern with all three, environment, development and peace/war, at the same time.

Security is the concept than can link all three together[11] because it presupposes invulnerability based on D and E, and a minimum of M – a defensive capability – more adapted to the nature of E and D. But just as development must not be at the expense of someone else's development, security must not be at the expense of someone else's security. To be safe others must also feel safe, if not they will fight the threat. The hope for this alternative security concept is that it generates processes that increase security. If I become less vulnerable and at the same time develop more defensive defense I do not reduce anybody else's security – I only increase my own. But if I do the opposite I certainly decrease the security of others. And hence my policy fails.

So far security has been seen from the point of view of the individual society. What about *collective security?* What can countries do together to enhance their security? Conventional security doctrine has a clear answer to this question: the formation of alliances – sub-regional, regional, even universal (UN) – with solidarity deep enough to make credible that an attack on one is tantamount to attack on them all. In other words, the creation of a security network, even a bloc, a macro-country. Through the logic of the military build-up in general this is likely to lead to a mirror phenomenon on the other side, meaning that blocs rather than countries will stand pitted against each other. The question is whether this merely means the transformation of the problems of the insecurity of countries to a "higher level" problem of insecurity of alliances, or whether something qualitatively new has been brought into the picture.

If the solidarity is operative, alliance-formation will at least transform individual country security to collective security. The individual country can probably be said to be protected against the danger of an isolated attack from the other side. An attack would have to develop into an attack on the alliance as a whole. But this is not the same as saying that collective security is higher than individual security. If individual security is *invulnerability + defensive capability − outside offensive capability,* then this formula is equally valid at the collective level. Hence, it becomes a question of what happens to these three components in the security formula under the transition from the individual to the collective level. The answer is not simple, but certainly does not necessarily indicate an increase in security.

As to invulnerability: it may be argued that an alliance of countries stands a higher *a priori* chance of being a stable eco-system, meaning not only self-reliant but self-sufficient, simply because it is larger. But this is not necessarily so. Whether for reasons of economic geography or economic policy, or both, the allied countries may be so similar in the international division of labor that their economic cycles are all extended into other parts of the world with complementary economies, paying for processed goods with raw materials and vice versa. As is argued above, eco-system instability combined with inequitable symbiosis between systems may easily translate into aggressive policies from either side. The combined destructive power of an alliance may then be behind such policies, adding considerably to the political and military weight a single country could place behind such threats or use of force. Which is only another way of saying that security can never be discussed in terms of the level of destructive power of various kinds alone. It must also be seen in a context of the structures in which this power is deployed – nationally and internationally – and this is what the vulnerability dimension tries to capture.

As to defensive/offensive capability: there are some strong reasons why an alliance will tend to have a lower defensive/offensive ratio than the sum of the individual countries. First, an alliance presupposes a higher level of mobility and range of the weapons systems in general for the simple reason that at least part of the total power may have to be used in one or more of the allied countries. Long distance transport/communication capacity becomes crucial, and for the other side any distinction between the capacity for use within and between alliances will carry little conviction – in general. Secondly, an alliance is not only a pact for mutual defense but also a pact for sharing costs and risks, including that of launching attacks, be it as first or second or nth strike. But this means, in principle, that a member country with only defensive capability may become a launching platform for offensive weapons used by other alliance members – such as long-range bombers or missiles (ballistic or cruise) with conventional or nuclear warheads, massive tank onslaughts, etc. One may say that this is in exchange for being protected by that power's offensive, retaliatory capability, the umbrella. But the net consequence is an increase in offensive capability. And then, *thirdly,* there is the argument alluded to several times above that centralized systems tend to demobilize defense capability locally because of dependence on the national center and nationally because of dependence on the international center, whether this is egalitarian or dominated by one power. Aware of this, the system may try to compensate by added offensive capability.

As to offensive capability on the other side: it will tend to increase as a result of his, in turn leading to reactive increases on the first side, and so on and so forth. The rest is known. Moreover, the most aggressive member may draw the entire aliance into a war.

Thus, there seem to be some reasons why alliances do not necessarily offer more security than non-aligned countries, although none of the arguments may be said to be absolutely compelling. However, they should make us ask the question again, in another way: Is there some other way of forging collective security than through alliance-formation, pitting friends against foes?

One answer would be: *by trying to help build security in others, not only in oneself.* If it is axiomatic that *security is indivisible,* in other words that my security also depends on your security, this should be a viable approach. More concretely, this would mean international co-operation across conflict borders, by making societies less vulnerable, and by building purely defensive capability of the kinds mentioned. With the high emphasis put above on the environmental factor in the vulnerability complex, this would call for even more environmental cooperation, not only for the obvious benefits in terms of production and human individual wellbeing (health in a broad sense), but also as an approach to security at the individual and collective levels. Such assistance will usually be extended to friends rather than to foes – even though the opposite would probably be more rational.

Conventional security doctrine tries to balance offensive capabilities against each other, either taking the vulnerability levels for granted or disregarding them. This class of security doctrines leads to *competition in offensive,* destructive capability, whereas the class of security doctrines based on high levels of invulnerability and defensive capability is completely compatible, indeed strengthened, through *cooperation.* Cooperative races would in and by themselves have distinct advantages over competitive races in a fragile world, particularly as this cooperative race would also be centered on how to build a world that could tend towards stable eco-systems at the global, national and local levels.

A world of only invulnerable/defensive societies would be greatly preferable to a world of only vulnerable/offensive societies. But what about a mixed world, if one assumes that there will be asynchronies in the transformation of societies or that some societies will successfully resist all attempts at transformation – much like the societies that held out long after others in practising colonialism? Would such a mixed world not be the most dangerous of them all? Would not the last offensive system have a comparative advantage like the last colonial power, the last slave-owner, the last trafficker in drugs, and so on? There is probably some truth in this. But it also depends very much on which country it is. A transformation process would either take place in a world climate where this becomes the thing to do, or itself create that climate. But this means that the last country would be the "odd one out", already marginal to the system, and this might tend to blunt its power. The physical power may be formidable, but faith in its legitimacy less – a little like the colonial power no longer believing in colonialism because there is (almost) nobody else around who does.

But all that notwithstanding, the main point would be that there is still a defensive capacity to counter such threats; and a high level of invulnerability – not a security reduction to zero. And there remains, of course, an alliance concept in everything short of offensive weapons, possibly even including non-provocative military support, which cannot be suspected of offensive functions. Economic, political, social and cultural (e.g. public opinion) support would be there. But no argument can serve to conceal the circumstance that humanity has now somehow managed to get itself into a corner from which there is no infallible escape – at the same time as the position in the corner is nonviable.

One important difficulty in the approach advocated is that some military might try to obtain both offensive and defensive arms, using the aversion to nuclear arms to build out conventional systems that, incidentally, are not necessarily defensive. Another problem is that the governments of transarmed countries could turn weapons that are defensive without into weapons that become highly offensive within. It is possible, if problematic, to make a distinction between weapons that can only be used offensively, abroad, and those that can only be used defensively, at home. But it is impossible to draw a distinction between weapons used at home against external and internal enemies of the government. The same weapons would be applicable in either case, by and large. In fact, offensive weapons may be useless against internal revolts (the case of Iran under the Shah) and in this there may be a factor of protection for the civilian population. A transarmament will expose the population unless the transformation to a more defensive weapons system is accompanied by a strengthening of society, both in the sense of reducing cleavages and in the sense of increasing local autonomy. In other words, a *Volksarmée* or something similar, a militia, would be the answer to this very important consideration, placing the arms in the hands of the people, not only of the government. The problem remains whether people will start fighting people, however.

Thus, the problem of finding a trade-off point between complexity and vulnerability is best solved through self-reliance at all organizational levels, and also in defensive capacity. The moment dependency chains of some length are created the complexity will increase. And so will the vulnerability.

4.4. The interface between environment, development and security

Sometimes one hears the argument that "environment has nothing to do with security", even in its institutional formulation: the former is a matter for UNEP, the latter for the Security Council.[12] This is the type of segmented thinking that cannot help being harmful to progress in the fields of both environment and security. For the linkages are numerous – as shown by the list of those touched upon in the present exploration:

(1) Wars are often over resources, i.e. over the environment, including area denial.

(2) Military activity is destructive of the environment, and uses eco-chains and eco-cycles for multiplier effect against environment.

(3) Destruction of the environment may lead to more wars over resources.

(4) If a country (including the human part) is a stable eco-system, then it is less vulnerable and hence more secure in the sense of
    – withstanding attacks better
    – less likely to attack others.

(5) If the local level (including the human part) is a stable eco-system, then the security of the country is enhanced
    – by being less vulnerable to attacks directed at the center
    – by being less vulnerable to internal imbalances.

(6) As the security of others also contributes to one's own security, helping to build stable eco-systems in others, nationally and locally, e.g. through international cooperation, promotes general security.

(7) The opportunity cost argument: resources spent on military activity could be used to strengthen eco-system stability all over.[13] Disarmament, even transarmament, could decrease the pressure on the environment.

Of these seven possible linkages the first three are hardly to be disputed. It should only be pointed out that (3) is not merely a logical consequence of (1) and (2), it points to the vicious circle that results from a war that destroys too much of the environment. The next three points are the positive version of the first three: if unstable eco-systems and deteriorating environments lead to war-like activity, it stands to reason that building stronger eco-systems, among other steps through control of pollution and depletion, would contribute to a decrease in war-like activity.

The following mechanism shows the validity of this: environmental deficits make a country more offensive because it is more vulnerable to attack and because it may wish to make up for the deficit by extending the eco-cycles abroad, diluting and hiding the pollution, getting access to new resources. The last point, (7), is only a corollary of the others. Together they add up to the conclusion that the environment is, or should be, a basic aspect of the security debate.

One can perhaps summarize as follows. We have been exploring three systems: environment, development and the military system. These are not mechanical systems. They are organic, goal-directed systems, the latter two to some extent steered by human consciousness. A reasonable goal for the environment system is ecological balance. A reasonable goal for the development system, although a very complex one, is the type of social development that leads to human development, which is a question of satisfying the "having" needs, and growth of the "being/becoming" needs. A reasonable goal for the military system is today the same as it has always been: the prevention of war and adequate defense should the war come. Are these goals compatible with each other and with security, meaning the probability of surviving reasonably intact?

Conventional security doctrine, based on offensive, retaliatory capacity, is in its consequences incompatible with all three, being highly destructive of the environment, a travesty of development, not necessarily preventing wars but possibly even provoking them, and incapable of delivering a reasonably intact society after the war. Admittedly there is a probability that it may prevent war, but if it does not the negative utility is so enormous that even multiplied by a low probability the product is highly negative.

An alternative security doctrine, based on a strong defensive capacity and a much less vulnerable society, has the advantage of having a stable eco-system and social and human development as conditions for security. Security, indeed, is based on the goals of the environment and development systems. Can it also prevent war and deliver adequate defense? Both these military functions would be based on the theory of "indigestibility", that a society thus organized would be highly unattractive because of its high *defense* capacity, as opposed to *retaliation* capacity. In addition such a country would base its security partly on being useful to other countries. Both military preparation and military action would be more compatible with environmental and developmental goals. The probability of deterrence through defense *may* be lower than that of deterrence through retaliation, although we do not really know. But even so, the negative utility of the destruction of environment and development would be so much less that the product of the two would certainly be very, very much lower in value. Actually this type of "cost-benefit" analysis is not even in order when the continued existence of civilization is at stake through conventional doctrines. The mathematics of simple products does not reflect this, but it is nevertheless a useful metaphor to conclude this exercise.

For instance, it is difficult to reflect the basic dilemma of nuclear deterrence: to be credible there has to be *some* willingness to use the arms, *some* willingness to engage in much of the omnicide they entail. But as these possible consequences become better known the resistance builds up, e.g. in the peace movement. And nuclear deterrence becomes less credible – *or,* there will be basic splits in the population over the issue. One more reason why alternative security doctrines are needed.

5. Towards recommendations

5.1. Armament, disarmament and transarmament

Continued armament and arms race in weapons of mass destruction in all likelihood leads but to war with mass destruction. The outcome is massively rejected by most people on earth. Most people when asked seem to want disarmament. Yet it does not come about. The United Nations has, in general terms, a vision:[1] D-Day (for disarmament) comes, there is political will in favor of it, the process of General and Complete Disarmament (GCD) takes place down to the level needed to maintain internal security (which may be quite a lot for some regimes), external security is organized under the United Nations Collective Security system, the resources liberated through the process are converted to civilian purposes in general and development in particular.[2] But it certainly has not happened this way. The reason may not *only* be lack of political will. It could also be that there is something wrong with the disarmament paradigm as indicated here – a possibility that will be explored in the next section.

Then there is a third paradigm competing for attention with the main trend armament paradigm and the major countertrend paradigm, disarmament: the transarmament paradigm. As it has been presented here (in 4.3 above) it differs from the disarmament paradigm in at least four significant ways:

(1) Transarmament can be undertaken by countries individually; it does not presuppose a general and complete political will.

(2) For transarmament the major distinction is between offensive and defensive weapons, assuming that all weapons of mass destruction are offensive (if for no other reason than because they are too destructive to be used at home).

102

(3) The military/civilian conversion problem is a minor one, since under transarmament there would still be a substantial military sector. Instead of the disarmament/development conversion in terms of resource transfer there could be a transarmament/development impact through structural change.[3]

(4) Much emphasis under transarmament would be placed on making societies less vulnerable, which implies some changes at various levels.

Let us then have a look at the type of recommendations.

5.2. Some disarmament recommendations

From the list of components used in 1.4 above to describe military *preparation* most of the theory of *disarmament* can be readily deduced, whereas the *laws of war* refer to efforts to limit military *action* by limiting destructive agents and/or destruction of targets. The concern here is with both the disarmament and the laws of war aspects of what may, perhaps, be called the general Geneva approach, which combines two interrelated approaches. Thus, a *no first use* pledge for certain types of arms (of mass destruction) in military *action* will have profound impact on the whole military *preparation*.

The general scheme would look something like this:

Figure 2. *The points of attack for disarmament measures*

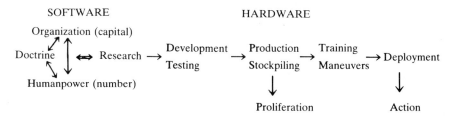

In principle there is one such chain for each weapons system (in 1.4). By conventional recommendations, then, I mean all recommendations that aim at eliminating or reducing/decreasing any one of these components *except doctrine*. By alternative recommendations I mean those that take as their point of departure the doctrine itself. Conventional recommendations tend to take the form of *disarmament* proposals; alternative recommendations the form of *transarmament* proposals. It should be noted that one set of recommendations by no means excludes the other. They complement each other.

Disarmament proposals are generally efforts to cut or control the chain above. This can be done by reducing standing armies, cutting their humanpower. However, instead of being labor-intensive the army then becomes capital-intensive, in line with the general transformation of production patterns usually referred to as modernization/development. So the next approach is often to propose budget control and cuts. However, instead of a capital-intensive army it may become research-intensive, also in line with general modernization patterns. In the military this would be the "bigger bang for the buck" or "more rubble for the rouble" approach. The next step would be to cut down on military research, but if that covers about 40% of the total research humanpower today, and a corresponding percentage of research facilities, it would be easy to hide some key research laboratory somewhere and continue the search. It looks as if the total disarmament approach is particularly unsuccessful exactly at this point, and since this is the starting point for the production chain, a necessary condition for the whole production of hardware remains uncontrolled.

But there are also ways of not fully developing military capacity, by aborting the chain:

> *doing research, but not development/testing*
> *doing development/testing, but not production/stockpiling*
> *doing production/stockpiling, but not training/maneuvers*
> *doing training/maneuvers, but not deployment*

The last proposal is the most modest, but perhaps also the most realistic one. It may be referred to as *distargeting* as opposed to disarmament. The hardware is there, it exists, people know how to use it, but it is no longer targeted, ready for use. The psychological impact of this type of withdrawal or non-implementation of the last logical step in the chain before action is what one would count on.

For all the steps mentioned above, however, the basic question is the time factor needed to restore the chain. It is obvious that the time factor is longer the closer one moves towards the beginning of the chain. Distargeting is more easily obtained, but also more easily undone. A real curtailment of research capacity would have a very significant impact, and would for that reason be considerably more difficult to obtain. For research capacity is the key to the qualitative jumps in military preparation, often referred to as the qualitative arms race. Without this production can continue along the old lines, contributing to a quantitative arms race which can be stopped through production stop (or moratorium). But if research continues qualitatively new chains can be opened parallel to the aborted one(s), not covered by previous agreements.[4]

To this should then be added the branching off of the chain known as proliferation, whether in the form of trade or secondary production (under license, with key components imported, etc.). The problem with non-proliferation agreements (with the efforts to curtail and control the general arms trade as a major, but special case) is the same as with economic boycotts/sanctions: they may encourage local, meaning primary, production. And denial of resources will probably lead to miniaturization, denial of labor to capital-intensive production and so on. In addition, it discriminates against have-not countries.

In general it must be said that this entire disarmament approach is wrought with considerable difficulties. If data alone are a guide the lack of success during fifty years of experience (1932–1982, with a break during the Second World War) should be enough to cause the approach to be regarded with less than optimism. If the preparation components (P) are multiplied with the action components (A) from 1.4 above so as to get a matrix P x A there are many jobs to be done (64 in our scheme). There are treaties covering some of them, at least normatively if not in fact, such as the conventions concerning biological weapons and environmental modification. But there are some very important reasons not to be too optimistic, or – if one prefers to put it that way – there is a theory that accounts for the empirical data about lack of success. To wit:

First, each country with a military system has an explicit or implicit security doctrine, to a large extent left untouched. Decision-makers feel that their country simply needs these things, if for no other reason because other parties have it (actio-ratio). There may be conflicts with one or more of these parties, and to have a military with software and hardware is the thing to do anyhow, part of growing up as a country, with the military roughly proportionate in size to the country's image of itself (structural compatibility). Hence they are more likely to use disarmament negotiations as a source of information than as a source of control of weapons systems.

Secondly, there are good reasons why disarmament processes will have to be mutual or have some element of mutuality. Complete unilateralism, put forward by very few, with no substitute such as militia or advanced police forces, would probably leave an entire country with the feeling that its identity was threatened in addition to its security. Few countries, if any, would be willing to do that *alone*. They might do so together with others. However: the moment the process is to be not only mutual but also balanced, the problem arises of how to compare and what to compare. No countries will have quantitatively and qualitatively identical weapons systems profiles. Gross comparisons of total destructive capacity will tend to be too speculative and controversial to serve as a basis for establishing the "balance". The comparison will tend to be component by component, leading to the image of parties with deficits in some components and excess capacity in others.

The consequence, if balance is aimed at, is more likely to be a making up for the deficits than a cutting down of the excesses followed by a cutting down altogether in a virtuous circle of disarmament. If the negotiations fail, this will serve as an incentive to catch up on the dimensions where there is a "gap". This tendency to catch up will itself make the negotiations fail. The maximum the parties will achieve will be a treaty for controlled armament, jointly catching up with each other – like the SALT approaches.

Thirdly, even if a process is mutual and balanced in terms of destructive power the countries would have to be almost identical for balance in the equally important field of invulnerability to obtain, including invulnerability of weapons systems although this, being more phsysical, is more easily operationalized. Disregarding invulnerability level makes the exercise very unrealistic; bringing it in is almost impossible.

Fourthly, if nonetheless a mutual and balanced process is agreed upon among negotiators in a Geneva process there is the question of wbether the MBCI complex at home will permit it to take place, given their vested interest and their usually very hardened security doctrine. They would at least insist on adequate control.

Fifthly, should a mutual, balanced and controlled process take place it is obviously much easier to cheat on one's own territory than to inspect somebody else's territory. This is a question of not only the asymmetry between a needle and a haystack, but also the question of whose needle, and whose haystack.

In spite of all of this, does it nevertheless make sense to argue for more efforts along the lines of the disarmament paradigm? The answer must be definitely positive. A norm in this field, produced by the appropriate machinery (usually UN), is nevertheless a contribution to the normative culture of the world, even if it is not adhered to, even if it leads to new forms of military preparation and/or action. The day may come when tension is reduced for some other reason; in that case the normative culture might surface and turn into a behavioral culture. It may be argued that then we would not need these agreements, but this is not correct. The agreements formulate relatively precise goals for the world system. At present strong processes and indicators point by and large in the opposite direction. But should these processes change there would still be a need for a goal, and such goals take time to sink in, to become internalized. The review processes uncover the extent to which the agreements have not become *institutionalized*, meaning that the control is not effective. But they may nevertheless be powerful mechanisms upholding the norms as such.

Of key importance would be *no first use* pledges for all weapons of mass destruction,[5] and *no use at all* pledges for as large areas of the world as possible. These areas do not need to be contiguous, nor do the countries in the areas have to agree at the same time. There is the *zone* model, whereby neighboring countries agree (and have the agreement guaranteed from the outside), and the *club* model, in which countries could join a club, maybe even by a domino process: one starts, the others follow.

To this should then be added deployment bans, and bans against training/maneuvers with weapons of mass destruction. But production freeze and stockpile reduction would also have to enter the picture, and then the problem of control becomes more difficult. If one pushes on, into development/testing, not to mention research, the control problem becomes (almost) insurmountable. Nevertheless, all the other, more superficial, measures would be useful by creating global norms, if not – yet, one might hope – global facts.

5.3. Some transarmament recommendations

This class of recommendations would have as their point of departure a change in security doctrine.[6] It would share with the disarmament approach the efforts to ban weapons of mass destruction, and weapons that cause unnecessary suffering. But it would go further into the range of conventional weapons, trying to weed out offensive weapons. At the same time it would actively *strengthen defensive defense measures,* perhaps even trying to create a world cooperative effort (under the UN) for truly defensive defense, including paramilitary and non-military measures. This would have immediate implications for the arms industry of the world. It would also have implications for alliances. A country opting for a defensive posture could not at the same time be at the disposal of another country with considerable offensive capability, but would have to decouple itself wholly or partly from such a country. In other words, a consequence of the transarmament approach would be a gradual dissolution of alliances.

But the second pillar in this alternative security approach is at least equally important: *building invulnerability.* This would have to be at the international, national, intra-national and local levels. Much of it can be phrased in terms of environment/development policies about which there is considerable agreement anyhow. A large part of the United Nations Environment Programme can be seen as a plan for enhanced world security and national security. The same applies to those development measures that aim at strengthening local and national productive capacity more than merely trade, and thereby very often patterns of dependency. To make people *more* able to live well off their local resources, well knowing that there will always be limits to them, by exchanging experiences as to how to do it, would seem a magnificent task for world cooperation. And much of it is already happening; it is a question of building on such positive trends.

The formula of "building invulnerability" actually implies a great deal of action to change inter- and intra-national social structures. A world and a country cut through by deep cleavages or contradictions will never be a secure place to live in. Hence, attention is drawn more towards the structural roots of the conflict and of the military preparations, including the arms races and military action. The disarmament approach has had a certain naiveté surrounding its claim that it is possible to control military systems that are obviously very deeply rooted in global and national structures, doing little or nothing about these structures. Any alternative security doctrine would have to take up this problem too, and it goes much deeper than merely trying to uproot MBCI complexes. But such efforts should also be seen positively as a contribution to security, not only as action against oppressive, dependency-creating structures.

Within countries this approach would call for more decentralization, local autonomy, and local self-reliance, economically speaking. It would also call for new approaches to problems of class relations, for instance more cooperative industries where the distinction between employer and employee would be considerably less sharp. And between countries the approach would call for a maximum of cooperation, but not of the type that creates dependencies, negative trade balances that have to be bridged by loans and debt-formation without end, among other reasons because of deteriorating terms of trade. If economic cooperation has this sort of consequence then maybe economic cooperation should recede into the background and cede a larger place to cooperation among scientists and experts, community to community, people to people, sports, culture, etc. Again two types of cooperation stand out: how to build defensive defense, and how to build less vulnerable societies. The experts here, incidentally, are obviously to be found more among neutral, non-aligned and Third World countries that in the NATO-WTO system. Hence the transarmament paradigm would also presuppose a certain reversal of the roles, with non-aligned countries playing a much more active part in security matters.

5.4. In lieu of conclusion

This is not the place to spell out the points made in the two preceding sections in any detail. This can only be meaningfully done in a concrete, political context. It is more a question of change of orientation than of concrete proposal-making – besides, most of the concrete proposals are obvious and already implemented by some countries. Where to look is quite clear; it is a question of wanting to look. To be afraid of nuclear arms is not enough.[7]

And this is not only a question of "political will". "Political will" presupposes that both goals and processes are relatively clear, it is just a question of the political timing being right so that the will emerges.

The point has been made above that the goal, GCD, is certainly acceptable but not very practical. But the UN image of the disarmed world may not even be acceptable because of the legitimation of "internal security forces" and the vagueness of UN collective security, in addition to the problems of conversion. And the process of disarmament negotiations does not seem very fruitful. *Hence it becomes a question of changing paradigms, not of political will inside an existing paradigm.*

This has happened before in the NATO-WTO system, which is the system of major concern in connection with the threat of a thermonuclear war. In the mid-sixties there was a tacit change of paradigm from security based on deterrence to security based on cooperation. *Détente* had this pattern at its center. How it came to an end during the late seventies we shall probably see with more clarity later. Suffice it to say that such changes are possible; what has happened once can happen twice. But last time there was no change in the military aspect of the security doctrine; it still rested on massively offensive weapons. Maybe the opportunity has now come for a new change of paradigm. For there is a limit to how long we can continue along present lines if we do not want our future to look like the next page:

THE WHITE DEATH

Appendix
The matrix approach

Three systems have been defined by their components: the *military system*, M; the *environment system*, E; and the *development system*, D. If we "multiply" the sets by each other, in the sense of making the cartesian products (like a cartesian coordinate system with all its points x, y is the "product" of the sets X and Y of numbers), we get nine products or *matrices;* starting with M since the focus is on military impact;[1]

	M	E	D
M	M^2	MxE	MxD
E	ExM	E^2	ExD
D	DxM	DxE	D^2

Each matrix is a scheme of relations between two components from the same or different systems, and what is put into cell i, j of the matrix would be some hypothesis about how element i in the first system in the product impacts on element j in the second system. We might also divide M into preparation and action, and D into human and social development and we would get 25 matrices, each giving an aspect of the total story. It should be noted that these matrices are not symmetric; the impact is not necessarily the same in both directions.

Some comments on the type of information demanded by these matrices, and offered when they are appropriately filled in:

M^2: the internal dynamics of the military system
E^2: the internal dynamics of the environment system
D^2: the internal dynamics of the development system

It is knowledge or hypotheses in general of this kind that makes it possible to talk about systems and not merely about sets of components. Some of this was explored in Sections 1.2, 1.3, 1.4 on E, D and M.

Then there are:

ExD: environment as a basis for development; how much development is possible with how much environment

DxE: development as a consumer of environment; how much environment is consumed by how much development

It should be noted that these are not the same problématiques. In ExD one would ask such questions as "Given an increase/decrease in grassland, how many more/fewer humans could be fed?" In DxE one would ask the opposite question, "Given an increase/decrease in the population, what would be the impact on grassland?" Or "Given an increase/decrease in the means of private transport, what would be the impact on grassland?" These are the typical ecodevelopment interfaces, very much explored in recent years. The first would see the environment as an independent variable, as something that can be changed by nature's self-destruction or by cultivating new environment. And the second would see development as the independent variable, posing the question of its impact on the environment. This is a crucial problématique in an era when development continually takes new forms but usually in the direction of increased pressure on the environment. Given the finiteness of the earth, and the difficulties with which nature renews herself, even withouth the production of biomass with a growth rate compatible with rising appetites, DxE tells the story of limits.

Then there are the key topics of the present analysis:

MxE: the impact of military activity on the environment; depletion, pollution and destruction of environment

MxD: the impact of military activity on development; opportunity costs, militarization, destruction

These are the matrices found in Tables 4, 5 and 6 in 2.2. and 2.3. It may be objected that this does not take into account possible positive impacts, but they are seen here as either negligible or subsumable under the broad heading of security, a special component of the development system, and then with an alternative M system.

Finally, there are:

ExM: improved environment possibly leading to more pre-
       paration; deteriorating environment possibly leading to
       more action

DxM: maldevelopment of society (under- and /or overdevelop-
       ment) leading to higher levels of military activity; deve-
       lopment possibly to less.

However, an analysis would not stop here, at the point of tracing connections merely between one element and another. One could use these nine matrices as raw material for the exploration of *chains* through three sets, and as there are three possible sets (M, E and D) for the first, second and third positions, we get a total of 27 possibilities. If the same set is in the first and the third positions these chains are called *cycles* – there are nine of them. They are particularly important because this is where the feared *vicious circles* may be located. Some examples, explored in the text:

DxExD: development leads to consumption of environment,
        which in turn imposes limits on development

MxExM: military action leads to deterioration of the environ-
        ment, which then leads to more military action

MxDxM: military action leads to maldevelopment of society,
        which then leads to even more military activity

And so on and so forth. The point to be made is that the approach chosen here forces us to explore all the possibilities. It does not guarantee that there is anything interesting everywhere; only that it may be worth looking into not only direct but also indirect effects (chains and cycles), and also through more than three sets.

There is still more to the matrix approach. A matrix can be added up horizontally and vertically, showing for MxE, for instance, which is the most dangerous military component and which is the most threatened environmental component. (Mathematically this is done by post-multiplication by a column matrix with 1's and pre-multiplication by a column matrix with 1's respectively.)

Chains and cycles can be explored through matrix multiplication. Thus, MxD gives the direct effects of military activity on development; (MxE) (ExD) gives the indirect effects on development via the effects on the environment. Here, however, a *caveat* should certainly be introduced. The indirect effect of M_i on D_k calculated this way would take us through the effect M_i has on all the E_j (j = 1,2, . . . n) multiplied by the effect all E_j has on D_k, adding it all up to a product sum. The question is whether an ordinary product sum as defined in arithmetic has any meaning in this context or whether we would have to go deeper into algebra to make sense. Matrix multiplication should be seen more as a heuristic metaphor than as an operation.

The problem is how to fill in the MxE and MxD matrices. For each component M_i we need information on effects on E_j, D_k in the other systems. These are bivariate relations, leading to the usual two questions of how the variables are operationalized, and what the functional relations can be said to be.

As to the military components: if the variable is a part of the *preparation* then it would be quantity of preparedness, e.g. manpower, military hardware produced, etc. If it is part of the *action* then some measure of the *yield* (Mt, kR, etc.) of the destructive action should be used.

As to the environmental components: the quantity of the component within a given unit of space (usually three-dimensional for atmosphere and hydrosphere, two-dimensional for lithosphere and biosphere) or, to allow qualitative reasoning, the quantity possessing a certain level of quality or more.

As to the developmental component: the quantity of human beings within a given area (e.g. a country) possessing a certain quality, such as survival, wellbeing, identity, freedom – for the space of human development. For the space of social development this becomes more complicated, among other reasons because development logic is incompatible with the logic of quantitative measurement (interval and ratio scales) and also calls for qualitative measurement (nominal and ordinal scales); like the logic for the development of individual human beings. Example: participatory structures abolished through martial law; learning curves; at some point there is a quantum jump.

For both E and D, then, destruction can be operationalized as the reduction in quantity of abiota, biota and humans, per space unit, generally, or of those possessing a certain quality such as "health" for humans. A basic problem with this approach is that it presupposes that all reduction in numbers is bad – an easy but simplistic position. To this may be countered that destruction is destruction whether to the good or to the bad. The rest is evaluation.

As to the functional relations: in general, the higher the degree of preparedness the more is taken from the E and D systems, posing the general problem not only of destruction, but also of opportunity costs. And the greater the yield, the greater the destruction. In other words, it can generally be assumed that the functional relations are monotone – never-increasing or never-decreasing functions.

But this leaves a considerable range of possibilities. Some of them are indicated in the figure:

Figure 3. *Some shapes of the destruction function*

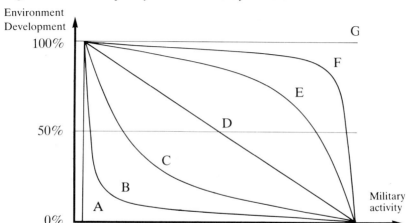

Destruction is to build *down,* hence the curve is shown as sloping downwards with increasing yield (the reference in the following is to military action rather than preparation but applies to either case). In the figure the level of total destruction is given as 0%.

The seven curves, or functions, range from one extreme to the other, from complete vulnerability/fragility triggered by a minimum level of military activity (A) to the function of complete invulnerability/robustness (G) where there is no destruction regardless of the level of military activity. Curve D is the simplest model, the linear relation, and B, C, E and F are in between. B and F have relatively clear turning-points after which there is very little/a great deal of effect of any additional military activity. Obviously military strategy is shaped by such considerations. Of particular importance is the 50% mark, where 50% of a given component is destroyed.

However, information is generally not available in this form. The data we have about the impact of ABC weapons are based on the Hiroshima/Nagasaki bombs and nuclear weapons tests, and on tests and some cases from the First and Second World Wars and the Indochina Wars. The question is how relevant these data are. We may have some points on the curves for some ranges and the danger is that we may even underestimate the deterioration/destruction. One can always try a linear extrapolation to estimate the impact of higher yields, for instance. But the problem is that we usually have insufficient data and/or theory to know with any level of certainty what the extrapolation function is – we only know that a linear function is the most simplistic of all assumptions about that function. More useful than many figures would be some good theory as to the functional shape, particularly whether the functions are of the A, B or F, G varieties, with triggering and turning points. Obviously, the empirical approach to this problem is what we have to avoid. But our experience is based on small bombs, Hiroshima-Nagasaki – bigger bombs may work qualitatively, not only quantitatively differently. They may cause apocalyptic, A-B type, effects.

On the other hand, the assumption of (rough) linearity, in other words a functional shape of the C, D, E varieties, may have the advantage that it does not incorporate too much of the higher order effects in our thinking. It is probably higher order effects, explored in the third chapter, that more than anything contribute to more extravagant functional shapes of the destructive variety. This means that more "well-behaved" functional shapes can be seen as a raw material basis for a more realistic analysis where higher order effects also enter. In general we would expect the curvature to increase with the length of the chain – pushing us towards A-B type scenarios.

For all these reasons it is probably safest to proceed with some rough categories rather than anything as demanding as functional shapes, for instance some rough categories in filling in the matrices and in commenting on them:

Most Important (functions A and B, particularly)
To Be Noted
To Be Watched
No Important Direct Impact (function G particularly)

Imagine that a set of *first order effects* of a military system on the environment and development systems has been established. For each component in the systems a function has been stipulated, generally monotone, between the yield of the military component and the destruction of that component, as if it were alone. The shape of the function is important: between the extremes of being absolutely vulnerable/fragile and absolutely invulnerable/robust all kinds of functional shapes can be imagined. The question is now how such first order effects relate to each other. This is a basic question in any system analysis, and the approach taken here is one that is developed for the particular problem we are dealing with, but it should also be applicable to other fields of inquiry.

The point of departure is the set of military components, M_1, M_2 . . . M_m and a set of eco-development components, $E + D$, C_1, C_2, . . . C_n. We assume the effect of any M_i on any C_j to be destructive, and symbolize this by $M_i - \to C_j$ (broken arrow); there are $m \cdot n$ such relations with more or less steep destruction functions. We can now distinguish between five types of different *higher order effects:*

(1) *Chains.* $M_i - \to C_j - \to C_k$ – particularly when C_j is a necessary condition for C_k so that the destruction of C_j becomes a sufficient condition for the destruction of C_k

(2) *Cycles.* There are two types that are of particular interest: $M_i - \to C_j \rightleftarrows C_k$ – the destruction of one component leads to the destruction of another, which then leads to more destruction of the first, and so on. $M_i \rightleftarrows C_j$ – the destruction of one component leads to more military activity and more destruction, etc.

(3) *Synergisms.* Two components are being destroyed by some military activity so that the destruction of one leads to even more destruction of the other.[2] Possible symbol: $(M_i - \to C_j) \Rrightarrow C_k$ – the destruction of C_j by M_i gives even more destruction of C_k by M_i. Or, in other words, the total destruction is more than the sum of the component destructions.

(4) *System composition.* The destruction rates will generally differ, and this will lead to changing composition of the system as the destruction proceeds. The elasticity, with $\triangle M_i$ cancelled, is an important

indicator of this, $\dfrac{\triangle C_j / C_j}{\triangle C_k / C_k}$, i.e. the ratio between percent changes, and a dimension-free number.

(5) *Recovery subsystem.* The recovery of a system will generally depend on some subsystem of the components (including their relations). Destruction of the recovery sybsystem will make replacement impossible, and destruction irreversible.

The term "breakdown" of a system should probably be used for this last type of destruction. Breakdown is much more than mere destruction of components, even many of them, and even to a considerable degree. Breakdown signifies inability to recover, even when some inputs are made from the outside. When this happens to a human being it is called death, and is characterized by its irreversibility. History has many examples of societies undergoing this fate, or being retarded.[3]

On what, more precisely, does the recovery depend? There seem to be two general answers, one in terms of the system itself – the components and their relations – and one in terms of some special subsystem that has repair/recovery as a specialized task within a total system division of labor.

The first approach is, by our definition, present in *mature* systems, meaning by that systems with a certain level of *diversity* (having several *types* of components), and a certain level of *symbiosis* among the components. This symbiosis, in turn, depends not only on the number of different components, but also on their relative frequency. Not only the elimination of types but the change of their relative frequency may make the system much less productive. The thesis would be that precisely the same holds for the human, social and world systems: their self-repair capacities are best at high levels of diversity and symbiosis, equitable symbiosis that is.

But in addition to this there is the specialized subsystem, like leukocytes in the human body, the health services and reconstruction agencies for social and even world systems.

Notes

CHAPTER 1.

1 "When a nuclear weapon is exploded above ground, the first noticeable effect is a blinding flash of intense white light . . ." (45, p. 49).

2 This dual nature of science, and by implication of technologies, serves as a point of departure for one important approach in this general field: the dual-purpose technology (28), the technology that can be used for good and for bad. In principle any technology can. The problem is under what conditions technologies are used for one or the other.

3 It may be objected that the nuclear war could start by accident. In a certain sense this is true, but it is hard to believe that nuclear powers have not done all they can to safeguard themselves against such an accident, which might also destroy themselves. If the system is sometimes reputed to be close to firing this may also be a calculated effect to instill fear in the other side, not an "accident". When it really is an accident we shall probably not hear about it or there will be efforts to cover it up. Moreover, the category is dangerous because it may lead to the idea that non-accidental, fully intended nuclear war is somehow more excusable. There is also a class aspect to the category: if heads of state desire to launch a war then it is politics; if lower ranks decide to do so, then it is an accident and they are portrayed as mentally deranged. What about the mental state of the highest ranks in the system willing to use such arms?

4 I had to introduce this term, like the term cosmosphere, to make for a more complete and semantically symmetric description of what this book is about. The homosphere is seen as comprising in its human settlements what is often called the *agrosphere* and the *technosphere.*

5 At this point there are many typologies. Usually they are based on a combination of temperature (arctic, temperate, tropical), degree of moisture (arid, desert, and oceans), and whether they are continental or islands. In the present book these distinctions are not pursued; see (60, ch. 1, III) or (41, ch. 3).

6 Westing (61, pp. 57f) uses "four somewhat overlapping yardsticks or indicators the magnitude and growth rates of which have led me to my pessimistic outlook for the future. On the other hand, I am sufficiently optimistic to believe that once the gravity of the situation becomes widely enough known, remedial action may well be forthcoming". The first is: the *gross global product* (GGP) "to serve as an indicator of global pollution levels. It is now known that when noxious substances, i.e., pollutants, are introduced into the environment, the affected eco-systems respond to such stress by reductions in species diversity, in biomass, in productivity, perhaps in stability or resilience, and, often, in resource values for humans". The second is *atmospheric concentration of carbon dioxide.* The third is species *extinction.* And

121

the fourth is *what happens to the earth's three major renewable natural resources,* i.e., "forests, grasslands, and fisheries". And he concludes: "one would expect a reduction in the disruption of the natural environment to the extent that the *arms expenditures* are reduced and *not* in the process diverted to civil uses. However, as the military sector shrinks, the civil sector is likely to experience an almost concomitant expansion" (p. 60). This is a key problem. For military preparation there is a civil sector conversion alternative; for military action fortunately none.

7 For an analysis of a Soviet view on the relation between environment and development, see (38). One important point is the optimistic note: "A strictly scientific approach considers as absolutely unfounded the ideas of "ecological malthusianism", which views man solely as a consumer of nature's resources and the carrier of some nature-destroying urge. In effect, however, man is, above all, a creative force. In the system of today's social production, he is the holder of the growing potential for increasing the wealth of nature and, in a broader sense, even for improving the organization of the biosphere" (p. 19). But what if he makes mistakes?

8 I am indebted to Arne Næss for this distinction between shallow and deep analysis of ecosystems. See his "The Shallow and the Deep in Long Range Ecological Movements," *Inquiry,* 1973, pp. 95–100.

9 This is the feedback loop given in Figure 1 above.

10 "Symbiosis is a mode of living, characterized by intimate and constant association or close union of two dissimilar organisms. Although the definition does not specify whether the results should be beneficial, indifferent or harmful to either partner, authors have tended to restrict the word to only mutually beneficial associations".

(17, p. 1027). Because of this ambiguity the term has to be made even more precise when applied to social systems: not only *mutually* beneficial, but (more or less) *equally* beneficial. Human history is full of cases of dominant parties who declare their "constant association or close union" to be mutually beneficial, such as slave-owners and slaves, husbands and wives – till the dominated party starts seeing it differently and acts accordingly.

11 I have in mind the many experiments trying to connect organic agriculture (polyculture) with solar energy, biogas converters, algae ponds, etc., drawing much more effectively on nature without disrupting natural systems.

12 Marxists would stress much more objective laws for societies. To me such laws are formulated in accordance with the cosmology or deep ideology of Western civilization – a reason why liberalism and marxism become so similar. The formulations then become ideology. They do not easily transcend the borders set by the cosmology; that would be "cosmopolitanism", a totally unrealistic assumption. Societies evolve within their cosmology till some type of disruption comes – and that is a rare event. That all societies should converge to the same point is totally improbable. For one exploration of this, see Galtung, Heiestad and Rudeng, "On the Last 2,500 Years in Western History, And Some Remarks on the Coming 500", *The New Cambridge Modern History,* Companion Volume, Cambridge University Press, 1979, pp. 318–61.

13 This is developed in Galtung, J., "The Basic Needs Approach", in Lederer, K., ed., *Human Needs; A Contribution to the Current Debate,* Hain, Königstein, 1980; pp. 55–125, a publication of the Goals, Processes and Indicators of Development Project.

14 This is explored in Galtung, J., *Why Does the Environment Deteriorate; And What Can Be Done About It,*

Paper for NGO Symposium on Environment and the Future, Nairobi, 2–7 May 1982 and in *Development, Environment and Technology*, UNCTAD, Geneva, 1979.

15 For one description of how brittle the eco-system already is and of how little it can afford the additional military insult, see Westing (60, p. 192)

16 The scheme for classification of weapons is derived from Robinson (41, p. 12).

17 The figures are from the UN study (45, p. 51); they are for fission bombs. For the hydrogen weapons the figures could be 55%, 38% and 7% respectively, and for a neutron bomb 40%, 25% and 35% – in other words an emphasis on radiation, particularly primary radiation (see also 22, p. 24).

18 But not always, as seen by the example of the internal arms race between army, navy and air force in the US (and probably also in many other countries).

19 The US Navy considers scuttling old nuclear submarines, but this seems to be less a disarmament measure than an (anti-) ecological measure: "the sea bed is a suitable place for reactors that are thousands of times more radioactive than the kind of low level waste commonly dumped off the Atlantic, Pacific, and Gold coasts between 1946 and 1970, when sea disposal of such radioactive material was allowed". (Carter, 4, p. 1495). The category of weapons that have become dangerous to the possessor could, perhaps, be added to the list.

CHAPTER 2.

1 The UN study reports (45, p. 5):
" . . . the total [of nuclear warheads in the world today] may be in excess of 40,000. In explosive power these warheads are reported to range from about 100 tons to more than 20 million tons equivalent of chemical high explosive. . . . The total strength of present nuclear arsenals may be equivalent to about 1 million Hiroshima bombs, i.e., some 13,000 million tons of TNT." After the study was written these numbers have certainly not decreased. Thus, Barnaby (11, p. 21) gives 50,000 warheads and one and a quarter million Hiroshima bombs.

2 Rotblat summarizes the technical and political aspect of civil defense as follows: (41a, pp. 117f):
"On the other hand, if the official policy of using nuclear weapons (for example the NATO policy to respond with nuclear weapons to a Soviet attack in Europe with conventional weapons) is to be credible, governments must show that they can cope with a limited nuclear attack by having taken steps to protect the civilian population. The result is a compromise, by which the governments are more likely to succeed in bluffing their own citizens than the enemy. . . . The only countries that have taken civil defense measures seriously, and have instituted a systematic shelter programme, even if not specifically designed for nuclear warfare, are the neutral states Sweden and Switzerland. They do not expect a direct nuclear attack, but are concerned about the fallout which may reach their territories from neighbouring countries."

3 Rotblat (41a) has a very thorough analysis of this.
A corresponding point is made by Geiger (15a, p. 960):
"Neither do they [OTA calculations] include such terrifying possibilities as blast-induced rupture of radio-active

123

waste storage containers and the consequent release into the environment of plutonium and other highly toxic or highly radioactive substances with half-lives in the thousands of years". It should be noted that Article 56 (1) of the Text of Protocol Additional to the Geneva Conventions of 12 August 1949, and relating to the protection of victims of international armed conflicts (Protocol I) adopted by the Conference on 8 June 1977, states that "Works or installations containing dangerous forces, namely dams, dykes and nuclear electrical generating stations, shall not be made the object of attack, even where these objects are military objectives, if such attack may cause the release of dangerous forces and consequent severe losses among the civilian population."

4 Thus, the scenario used in the special AMBIO issue for SSDII (1982, No. 2–3) involves a total of 14,737 warheads and a total megatonnage of 5750.3 Mt, of which 5576.9 would be used in the Northern Hemisphere (97%) and 173.5 Mt (3%) in the Southern Hemisphere.

"An all-out exchange utilizing all existing weapons would not at present be lethal globally, but a continuation of the present rate of weapons production and stockpiling might make that capability real in as little as 20 years." Also see (8, pp. 122–23).

6 There are many ways in which one could arrive at scenarios for a possible nuclear war in a more systematic way, but they would all assume that where a conflict breaks out is one thing, and where it takes nuclear form is quite another. Of most concern to people in the NATO-WTO area is, of course, the possibility of Euro-tactical, Euro-strategic or inter-continental nuclear warfare. It is generally seen as unlikely, today, that it should be triggered by conventional warfare in the NATO-WTO area. But it could be triggered by conventional conflicts elsewhere that develop into nuclear war or come into the NATO-WTO area, e.g. by a country in that area being involved in a "local" conflict and wanting to involve others by extending the conflict.

7 For an overview of the military consumption of natural resources, see Hveem and Malnes (19). As the authors say, data are largely unavailable, however. Also see Huisken (18).

8 Lumsden mentions these categories of land use by the military (32, pp. 40f): "training areas, fortifications, storage areas, airfields and harbours, military cemeteries . . . areas . . . for testing nuclear weapons, missiles and other munitions . . . military border zones". He obtained data from 13 countries (six of them NATO, five WTO, but not the Soviet Union), and the "thirteen countries between them use more than 14 million ha for military purposes (including more than 1 million ha in foreign countries)". He also gives an example of the space required: "Training with air-to-air missile can require an area of 225,000 hectares. And even more land is required for testing missiles and weapons of mass destruction." (32, pp 44–45).

9 Lumsden (32, pp. 45–47) summarizes some of his findings in four propositions:

As the size of armed forces increases, so do the demands for larger land areas.

As the level of technological sophistication increases so do the demands for larger land areas.

As the organizational level of maneuvers increases (from company to battalion, brigade or division), so do the demands for land.

As the population moves into the cities, the armed forces are moving out into the countryside.

All four processes are taking place in the world today, and as a consequence the pressure on the land increases.

10 "The North American Air Defense Command (NORAD) is charged with the responsibility of tracking man-made objects in Earth orbit [from about 100 to about 22,000 miles]. Since NORAD's purpose is to identify objects that may represent a threat to national security, it is most interested in the largest objects, but objects as small as four inches in diameter are also tracked. NORAD currently monitors the orbits of the approximately 5,000 objects in Earth orbit." (24, p. 14).

The UNEP report (49, p. 36) gives the number of "military or part-military satellites launched since 1957 to 1,601 or about 75 per cent of all the satellites launched."

For a survey of military uses of space, see (10). For satellites alone he quotes an official US source (7) as saying that the two super-powers in the years between 1957 (Sputnik I was launched in October that year) and 1980 launched 2077 satellites; 427 of 760 or 56% of those launched by the US being military, and 890 of the 1317 launched by the USSR, among them many anti-satellite satellites (p. 259).

11 Of all of these effects there is hardly any doubt that the one that has caused most concern has been the testing of nuclear weapons. "The annual deposition of fission products from nuclear tests reached a peak in 1963, but since the partial Treaty Banning Nuclear Weapon Tests in the Atmosphere, in Outer Space and Under Water of 5 August 1963, this source of radio-nuclides has been steadily declining, although there have been a few small peaks superimposed on the decreasing trend as a result of atmospheric tests of nuclear weapons by countries which were not signatories to the Treaty" (52, paragraph 16, p. 5).

"For the world population this would lead to one death for each kiloton fission exploded. With this measure all past atmospheric tests could be equi-valent to about 150,000 premature deaths worldwide, and approximately 90 per cent of these would be expected to occur in the Northern Hemisphere." (45, p. 86).

Nazarov gives this estimate of the effect of testing (36, p. 39): "Before 1963 the total power of nuclear bombs exploded in the atmosphere was 510 megatons. Now it is 540 megatons. The environment received 11.5 megacuries of strontium 90 and 18.5 megacuries of cesium 137. Is it much or little? When one operates with complex physical values, the real essence of phenomena is involuntarily lost. Therefore, a simple example may serve as an illustration. Now the strontium and cesium released into the atmosphere have almost fully fallen on the surface of the Earth. Every square kilometer in the northern hemisphere has about 100 milicuries of cesium 137 and 50 milicuries of strontium 90, which means that on each square meter in any country of that hemisphere there explodes every second and decays 5 thousand radioactive man-made atoms which had never existed in nature. And that condition will last for many decades".

12 " . . . a very disproportionately great share of all research and development [R and D] throughout the world, indeed, of all scientific effort, is directed toward weapon and other military advancement. At least one fourth of all R and D in the world at present is carried out for military purposes" (61, p. 60). "It has been estimated that the average military product is some twenty times as research-intensive as the average civil product" (51, p. 165).

13 "The levels of contamination [of fresh-water systems following a nuclear war] would increase in the order: ground-water reservoirs, lakes, rivers, rainwater. In regions exposed to early fall-out rainwater would be a deadly poison for at least two weeks following such a war. . . . The number of

deaths and sicknesses due to fresh-water contamination would be large, but small in comparison with those due to the severe and long-lasting contamination of the food chain, and to the many other effects of nuclear war". (63).

14 Figures from Westing (11, p. 59).
For estimated damage on various ecosystems and parts of ecosystems as a result of a 20 Kt and 1 Mt bomb exploded in the troposphere and at the surface respectively, see Westing (58, pp. 16 and 17), also (62, p. 270). For an estimate of the impact of a 1 Kt neutron bomb exploded in the troposphere see Westing (62, p. 271).
The UNEP report states (49, p. 37): "It is estimated that detonation of a one-kiloton [neutron] bomb 200 metres above the ground will cause death to a wide range of micro-organisms over an area of 40 hectares, to many insects over 100 hectares, to many amphibians and reptiles over 330 hectares, to many species of higher plants over 350 hectares, and to many species of exposed mammals and birds over 490 hectares."

15 " . . . women are slightly more susceptible to immediate effects than men, and individuals of both sexes below 10 years old and above 49 years greatly more at risk, yet most groups will suffer in proportion to their composition. The only marked changes will be a relative absence of those (i) aged above 49 years, and (ii) below 10, at the time of attack. This high mortality-rate among children will exacerbate the effects of the baby-vacuum between ten and thirty years afterwards, when the number of young, productive adults in the population will be greatly reduced, and there will be a particular problem at, say, forty years after the attack, when a 'large' number of old people will require support from an extremely small productive age-band." (5, p. 233).

16 In general, for the impact of conventional warfare on the environment, see Westing (11, pp 64 ff), where he discusses the war damage in temperate and tropical zones, using World War I and II as examples of the former and the Second Indochina War as an example of the latter, " . . . the first war in modern history in which environmental disruption was an intentional and substantial component of the strategy of one of the belligerent powers. In an attempt to subdue a largely guerrilla opponent, the USA pioneered a variety of hostile techniques . . ."
The UNEP report states that "the Second World War caused a short-term reduction of 38 per cent in the agricultural productivity of 10 nations; recovery progressed at about 8.3 per cent per annum" (49, p. 36).

17 This point is made by Westing (11, pp. 68–69) comparing US military action in World War II, the Korean War and the Second Indochina War. "US battle intensity as measured in terms of the monthly number of US combat fatalities dropped progressively from each of these wars to the next, in the ratio of 15:2:1, respectively. Combat fatalities among the forces opposed to the USA followed a remarkably similar trend, also exhibiting a ratio of 15:2:1. [But] US munitions expenditures were in the approximate ratio of 1:5:7 [and] per enemy soldier killed in the even more startling ratio of 1:6:18". A tremendous excess for non-human targets; in short, for ecocide.

18 Species selective mortality may overload the food chain. Particularly important are the weapons that have a biospecificity for the plant species that dominate the primary production in a region, and hence also the soil cover. Specificity is important because weapons that are too unspecific cannot be used to obtain specific goals, hence are less useful politically.

19 The major study in this field is the Thorsson Report (51).

20 Whether this is "good" or "bad" depends on the societal goal. Military systems may be models of individual mobility in societies permitting no mobility at all, such as caste societies. And military systems that come out of a guerilla tradition may be models of horizontal relations in societies with very steep stratification systems, of the caste or class varieties.

21 For one example of opportunity cost calculations, see (48, p. 3):
"Examples of military vs. civilian costs:
–$500,000 is the cost of one tank – or equipment for 520 classrooms
–$20 million is the cost of one jet fighter – or 40,000 village pharmacies
–$100 million is the cost of one destroyer – or electrification for 13 cities and 19 rural zones with a population of 9 million
–In two days the world spends on arms the equivalent of one year's budget for the United Nations and its specialized agencies".
Half of the world's military expenditure in one day is sufficient for a full programme for control of malaria (according to WHO). 1,500 million people – nearly 40% of the world's population – have no effective medical services, nearly 570 million people are severely undernourished, about 3,000 million lack access to safe water, and nearly 750,000 die each month from water-borne diseases. About 800 million are illiterate and nearly 250 million children under the age of 14 do not attend school.

22 Of all these effects it is quite possible that the use of scientists for military rather than developmental purposes is the one that has struck people most, for so many of the other effects (e.g. the opportunity costs) would seem to follow from it.
"At the present time, there are barely a million scientists and technicians . . . roughly 400,000 individuals are working on military projects . . ." (11, p. 9).
Khozin analyzes the impact the military has on science and technology and on the environment, but sees it as a characteristic of capitalist countries:
"Ces deux phénomènes–militarisation du progrès scientifique et technique et attitude purement utilitaire a l'égard de la nature–ne sont pas nouveaux dans les pays capitalistes" (25, p. 111, in his chapter "La course aux armements est néfaste pour la nature"). It is hard to believe that these phenomena should not also occur in state socialist countries.
Novikov summarizes negative impacts of military activities in peace time: "the functioning of the war industry, whose production base is very closely linked with heavy industry producing major pollutants, and which in many countries is less affected by ecological controls; the testing of weapons and military equipment, military exercises and training, troop movements, their maintenance at military bases; the collection, storing, transportation and destruction (dumping) of lethal by-products of the war industry, and of 'surpluses' of chemical weapons and other weapons of mass destruction" (39, p. 18).

23 It is important here to compare the non-aligned/neutral countries in Europe with the countries that are members of the alliances. They are not so very different in terms of social, political and economic variables. They differ above all in terms of military expenditure, the non-aligned/neutral to a large extent spending less per capita (with the exception of Switzerland), and may also differ in level of security – probably by having a higher level of security since they threaten nobody.

24 Overmilitarized Iran collapsed, as is well known, whereas undermilitarized

Germany and Japan did not seem to do badly economically after the Second World War. If Germany now does less well it is not because it has not devoted more of its resources to the military sector, which is mainly unproductive.

In one analysis (34, p. 953) this point is expressed as follows, referring to the commonly found calculation of military costs by presenting the budgets of a Department of Defense as 5–8% of the gross national product. "This mode of reckoning, however, is flawed on two counts: first, the budget of the Department of Defense is only a part of the total military outlay by the federal government; and second, the more critical relationship is between the cost of the military effort and the annual new quantity of domestic capital formation in the United States. . . . The United Nations assembled data for the early 1970s, showing that, on an average annual basis, the ratio of military budgets to domestic capital formation was 2 percent in Japan, 13 percent in Germany, and 32 percent in the United States (47, p. 82). The markedly higher concentration of the US fresh potential capital in the military sphere goes far to explain the contrast between the modern, burgeoning technological strength of Japanese and German industries, and the sparkling quality of public amenities and services in the great cities of Japan and Germany, compared with the United States. The controlling consideration is the fact that from an economic standpoint the military use of capital yields no product which enters into consumption or can be used for further production. Accordingly, military activity yields no economic use value; and the concentration of a nation's capital potential in the military area has the necessary result of limiting economic productive capability of every sort." "Detailed studies of the decline of once competent U.S. industries,

supported by solid statistical analyses, confirm that the sustained military-priority use of capital and technical brains is the prime cause of the decline in U.S. productivity growth. Inflation plus unemployment have been the bitter fruit of the lowest productivity growth of any industrialized country" (34, p. 954). Of course, the military budget sustains military and civilian families in the armed forces as well as those engaged in military production directly and indirectly, but this could have been achieved with the same amount of capital for production "which enters into consumption or can be used for further production."

25 The point is important, not so much because of the usage of these terms "higher" and "lower" to describe plants and animals, as because of the transfer to the field of human societies. The more complex and differentiated society is often seen as "higher", but it follows from this type of analysis that it is also more vulnerable. However, as will be explored in Chapter 4, there is a relation between being vulnerable and having offensive weapons systems. By implication, this use of the terms goes far to justify the development of offensive weapons, since they are in the hands of "higher" societies.

26 Martin (33) puts it this way: "The following areas would be relatively unscathed by direct effects, unless nuclear attacks were made in these regions: South and Central America, Africa and the Middle East, South Asia including India, Australia, Oceania and large parts of China". And: "Nuclear war is the one source of possible deaths of millions of people that would affect mainly white, rich, Western societies (China and Japan are the prime possible exceptions)". And he observes: "White Westerners may tend to identify their own plight with that of the rest of the world, and hence exaggerate the threat of destruction wreaked on

their own societies into one for all of humanity."

27 "The immediate effect of the 188 target, 167 Mt nuclear strike will be fatalities in the order of 6 to 8 million and seriously injured of between 10 and 16 million. At one month after attack there should be 31–39 million able-bodied survivors. The mortality rate *per se* does not appear to be a central issue for 'survival' and it cannot be calculated with any degree of accuracy" (5, p. 238).

In his article "What happens if SS-20 missiles are used against military targets in Norway". Höivik (20) emphasizes that even if there is no attack on Norway an attack on Britain could result in very many casualties from fallout if the wind blows from south-west. In his scenario for a counter-force Soviet attack against Norway Höivik operates with 5 SS-20, each one with three warheads of 150 Kt each against military targets, and 10 SS-4/5 with one warhead of 1 Mt each against radar stations. Iversen (22, p. 60) uses the same scenario and arrives at the very tentative conclusion of 300,000 killed and 600,000 seriously wounded, among them 100,000 with serious burns. It should be pointed out that this is not a very heavy attack and involves only 5 of the 10 known COB airports in Norway (Iversen, 22, p. 52).

28 See the UN Study (45, p. 77). Also, see OTA study (8, p. 140).

According to one study (14, p. 3) by the National Security Council the number of people killed in a US-USSR nuclear conflict would be 140 million in the United States and 113 million in the USSR.

29 See Höivik (20).

30 For a forceful argument against the notion that the apocalyptic vision is necessary to mobilize people, see Martin (33). On the other hand, there are people who are said to shrug their shoulders at the death of "only" 10–20% of humankind.

31 "It is probable that there will be a mass exodus from the city peripheries, but these survivors of blast and heat will die from injuries sustained and/or exposure to lethal radiation. Medical services will be largely unavailable at this time and those hospitals still in operation will be quickly overwhelmed" (5, p. 238).

32 Quite important here is the current tendency towards big hospitals and towards the centralization of the health services in general. Not only are they located in bigger cities, which in themselves are vulnerable, but the services are also increasingly vulnerable, dependent as they are, for instance, on electronic equipment.

33 Schell (42, p. 35) mentions some of the "necessary equipment for an effective shelter": "adequate shielding from radiation; air filters that would screen out radioactive particles; food and water to last as long as several months; an independent heating system, in places where winters are severe; medical supplies for the injured, sick and dying, who might be the majority in the shelters; radiation counters to measure levels of radiation outdoors, so that people could know when it was safe to leave the shelter and could determine whether food and drink were contaminated; and a burial system wholly contained within the shelter, in which to bury those who died of their injuries or illness during the shelter period". In this list Schell actually manages to portray the irrealism, or *surrealism* (I am indebted to Jan van Ettinger for this point), of nuclear war and protection against direct attack by describing the plight of the sheltered, not only the unsheltered.

34 Most people in the West would, one assumes, prefer to be neither red nor dead. The question is how one's security doctrine, given a choice only between these two alternatives, tilts the answer. There can be no doubt that a

doctrine of "massive retaliation" or the more modern versions of the same, is a "better dead than red" doctrine as nuclear weapons will be used even as a response to a conventional attack that looks successful (otherwise there would be no reason to respond with nuclear arms). But nuclear responses will, it seems, invite a massive nuclear counterattack from the other side – and this is known, although, possibly, not fully believed. This in itself, the poverty of options in case of crisis, is an argument against current security doctrine.

35 According to deKadt (23) if urban areas and particularly the commercial city centers are destroyed, this means the destruction of the central system of banking and credit, finance and insurance, many technical and organisational specialists and the professions in general.

36 There is actually surprisingly little debate about this aspect of current strategic doctrine, the higher invulnerability offered to some elite and certainly not to the whole population.

37 See note 11 above for some data about the contamination brought about by *testing,* for the *whole* world (although mainly for the Northern hemisphere). We are dealing here with real *war,* and a much more limited area.

38 Article 55 of the Text of Protocol Additional to the Geneva Conventions of 12 August 1949, and relating to the protection of victims of international armed conflicts (Protocol I) adopted by the Conference on 8 June 1977 states that "Care shall be taken to protect the natural environment against widespread, long-term and severe damage. This protection includes a prohibition of the use of methods or means of warfare which are intended or may be expected to cause such damage to the natural environment and thereby to prejudice the health or sur-.vival of the population. Attacks against the natural environment by way of reprisals are prohibited." In practice this is a prohibition of nuclear arms.

39 Article 53 (a) of the Text of Protocol Additional to the Geneva Conventions of 12 August 1949, and relating to the protection of victims of international armed conflicts (Protocol I) adopted by the Conference on 8 July 1977 states that it is prohibited "to commit any acts of hostility directed against the historic monuments, works of art or places of worship which constitute the cultural or spiritual heritage of peoples". Not so easily implemented if nuclear arms are used, but with adequate dispersion of such monuments it many also be seen as outlawing nuclear warfare. Also see Westing (60, p. 201).

40 One characteristic of the "survivalists" is given by Dragdahl (9). "In Western Europe the threat has created a peace movement of people who together appeal to their political authorities. In the US movement the key words are individual salvation and distrust of established authorities." This was written before the US anti-nuclear peace movement really emerged in April 1982, but still points to something essential, clearly expressed in the handbook for survivalists, *Life after Doomsday,* by Bruce D. Clayton.

41 Galtung, J., *Development, Environment, Technology,* UNCTAD, Geneva, 1979 spells out this in some detail in Chapter 1.

42 *Ibid.,* Chapter 5.

43 This would be the Brandt Commission proposal in reverse.

44 To counteract guilt a number of mechanisms would be available:
–"The other side started."
–"I was simply obeying orders."
–"There were many of us taking the decision and launching the attack."
Thus, the combination of blaming the other side, vertical subordination and collectivist submersion will serve to exonerate the individual, and these

structures are already created in peace time.

45 Clarke makes the point (5, p. 240) that "mass death will have broken the 'death taboo' " – an important point because this is what would condone violence. In the presence of very many corpses one more or less would seem less significant, particularly if the person already shows symptoms of being a radiation victim.

46 Daniel Ellsberg makes this point in his book *Papers on the War*, Pocket Books, Simon Schuster, New York, 1972, p. 295.

47 The UNEP report (49, p. 36) states that "more than 100 kg of dioxin was inadvertently disseminated as an impurity in one of these defoliants, and this substance has since been linked to human birth defects and miscarriages and to liver cancer". It went on for so many years that it was hardly inadvertent, however. Veterans Administration, *Review of Literature on Herbicides, Including Phenoxyl Herbicides and Associated Dioxins,* Vol. I, Washington, 1980.

48 Westing reviews the cases of U.S. accusations of the Soviet Union "employing harassing, incapacitating, and lethal anti-personnel agents in this endeavour [Afghanistan] against both military personnel and civilian populations"; "Laos together with Viet Nam of employing chemical weapons against anti-government among (Meo) tribespeople since 1974"; "Kampuchea together with Viet Nam (and again in collusion with the Soviet Union) of employing chemical weapons in recent years against the insurgent Pol Pot and Khmer Serei forces holding out in Western Kampuchea"; and that "Viet Nam in collusion with the Soviet Union had been for about five years and was continuing to employ a number of chemical agents, among them toxin agents, in both Laos and Kampuchea". In all cases evidence seems to be inconclu-

sive. If these terrible arms had really been used on an operational scale one would have expected evidence to be available. Westing, A., "Chemical and Biological Weapons; Past and Present", Paper prepared for the American Association for the Advancement of Science, Washington, 3–8 January 1982.

According to an article in the *International Herald Tribune* (26 January 1982, p. 1), "U.S. sprayed Herbicides on Laos", "the United States secretly sprayed herbicides on Laos during the Vietnam war" – information obtained by the National Veterans Task Force on Agent Orange. The IHT tried to have the story confirmed by key decision-makers at that time, but as pointed out in a letter to the editor some days later (IHT, 8 February 1982, "Legacy in Asia") all of them had "simultaneous memory failure over the recommendations and orders they signed for the illegal and secret spraying of Laos and South Vietnam with poisons in the early 60s".

49 "Science fiction writers have speculated, for example, that in the aftermath of a nuclear war, the survivors would place the blame on 'science' or on 'scientists', and through a combination of lynching and book-burning eliminate scientific knowledge altogether. There are cases in history (or rather in archaeology) of high civilizations that simply stopped functioning (although people survived physically) after some shattering experience" (8, p. 115). According to one author, during the Black Death of the fourteenth century there was "general demoralisation and social breakdown, a mood of misery, depression and anxiety" (13, p. 159).

50 As is well known, this injunction is not followed. As the executive director of UNEP, Dr Mostafa Tolba, told the UNEP Session of a Special character, May 10 1982 (in Nairobi): "Take action now or face disaster". (If not) "by the end of the century an environmen-

tal catastrophe which will witness devastation as complete, as irreversible as any nuclear holocaust" *International Herald Tribune,* 11 May 1982.

51 For an evaluation, probably too conservative, of the potentials of these "new weapons", see the UN Study (45, p. 43, § 117–19).

52 For one particular city council's reaction to the concept of evacuation into host communities, see (26). In the pamphlet published by them citizens are urged to begin discussions at home, in church, at school. For a description of the Civilian-Military Contingency Hospital System (CMCHS), see (55). The first assumption is "We assumed that there would not be an attack on the United States homeland" (55, p. 1). This may be seen as either unrealistic or as a general signal of a strategy that has been successful so far – there has been no attack on the United States homeland. The war has been limited to somewhere else (e.g. Europe).

CHAPTER 3.

1 The UNEP report (49, p. 36) states that "in South Viet Nam chemical herbicide completely destroyed 1,500 square kilometers of mangrove forest and caused some damage to 15,000 square kilometers more, and natural recovery is proceeding slowly".

2 Robinson emphasizes the role of forests (41, p. 53): "So powerful is the momentum which forests may impart to the cycling of nutrients, and so strong may their influence be on the hydrological and meteorological conditions of a region, that their importance within an ecosystem, and hence their loss, may be felt over an area far exceeding that which is actually forested. There have been innumerable instances in history, which continue to repeat themselves even now, of deforestation being succeeded by widespread land degradation and improve-

rishment of the region, amounting, in some cases, to desertification and other forms of ecological disaster».

3 "It has been estimated that 10,000 Mt would pollute the stratosphere with 10^7–10^8 tons of material" (45, p. 80).

4 "As low a dose as 100 rad could be prohibitive to the body's own capacity for recovery from thermal burns and might hence cause death in the cases where the person would otherwise have recovered from his burns" (45, p. 169).

5 (45, p. 170).

6 "The 1°C cooling could severely hamper wheat growing in Canada and parts of the USSR, for instance, due to a reduction of the number of frost-free days" (45, p. 80).

7 ". . . at a dose of 200 rad such wounds [from flying glass or wood, broken bones, cuts and internal injuries] might be fatal – through infection or loss of blood – where they would otherwise have healed" (45, p. 169).

8 "Even in winter there would still be some insect problem since these, of all animals, have an enormously high resistance to radiation and can be expected to multiply given the absence of mammal predators" (5, p. 220). "Finally, note that my title asks 'Can we *survive'*, not 'Can we *win* a nuclear war'. In a major exchange between the superpowers the only possible winners would be the cockroaches, which are allegedly much less sensitive to radiation than mammals. Any major city, hit by a megaton weapon, will be totally destroyed – almost instantly set ablaze by the heat, leveled by the blast, completely disorganized by the ensuing firestorm and destruction of all transport and medical facilities" (12, p. 38).

9 The key epidemics will probably be tetanus, typhus, hepatitis and tuberculosis (5, p. 221): "It is also entirely possible that more serious epidemics will develop, not excluding plague spread by rats, whose existence in sew-

ers (and beneath London in the 'Underground') will not be greatly disturbed by the attack itself but who will be offered an ample food source and ideal conditions in its aftermath. A report in The *Guardian* of 20 October 1976 stated that 'the entire Leicester Square area is infested with rodents. They are particularly fond of the Piccadilly Tube Line, probably because of its warmth whilst many buildings in this area are infested with mice' "(5, p. 222). To this factor one might add: ". . . the depletion, caused by ionizing radiation, of certain corpuscles in the blood which produces a state of general weakness and, in particular, a degradation of the immunological defense in the body" (45, p. 169).

10 For an analysis of this type of system within and between countries, see Galtung, J., "A Structural Theory of Imperialism", *Essays in Peace Research,* Vol. IV, ch. 13, Ejlers, Copenhagen, 1979.

11 For an analysis of this see Galtung, J., O'Brien, P. and Preiswerk, R., *Self-Reliance,* Bogle d'Ouverture, London, 1980, or Galtung, J., *The True Worlds,* Macmillian-The Free Press, New York, 1980, particularly Chapter 9.

12 "In the same way that the Second World was follwed by a "baby-bulge' so this nuclear war and its aftermath will result in *baby-vacuums* – an absence of new citizens" (5, p. 231). "Many women pregnant at the time of the attack will be dead and most of the irradiated survivors will have spontaneously aborted; in any case, the foetus is between twenty and sixty times more sensitive to radiation than the normal adult" (5, p. 231-2).

13 "In the context of hardship and deprivation, severely retarded physical and mental growth was not uncommon among the A-bomb fetal victims – especially in the form of microcephaly. . . . a condition wherein an individual's head size develops small in proportion to body size, and symptoms of mental abnormality appear. Among the various causes of this condition, one is irradiation of the fetus in the womb." (6, pp. 449f). "They barely manage to serve as workers' helpers or do odd jobs for sympathetic employers. They tend to be slow-moving and short on understanding and judgment; and as they can hardly perform normal duties, their pay is extremely low" (6, p. 453). Also see (60, p. 60).

14 "There is no real evidence to support the popular belief that nuclear war would be followed by human mutation on a large scale – that humanity would change its shape" (5, p. 232). And then: "It is certain that the radiation derived from a nuclear war would cause mutations in surviving plants and animals; it is possible that some of these mutations might change the ecosystem in unpredictable ways, but this seems unlikely." (8, p. 115). But: "We found no clearly statistically significant effects of parental exposures on the offspring characteristics which we studied, but the various indicators of possible genetic damage all are in the direction expected if an effect was indeed produced. On the basis of the enormous body of data concerning the genetic effects of radiation on experimental organisms, we feel there can be no doubt that some genetic damage was sustained by the survivors of the bombings" (37). Barnaby and Rotblat mention (2) some possible explanations why there has been no genetic damage in the survivors: the number of survivors with sufficient radiation doses received was too low to produce a sufficient number of children to show statistically significant genetic effects; the research methods were not good enough; mutations may show up in later generations; there may have been a large number of spontaneous abortions.

15 In an early study (40) the effect of a 56 Mt on Massachusetts, including down-

town Boston, is calculated to be "Over the entire state, including the Boston area, over 1,300,000 will die immediately, over 2,300,000 will be injured, and of these about two-thirds will die". The study then focusses on the health sector and concludes that (on the basis of 1950 census figures) 4,800 of Boston's 6,560 physicians would be killed and 1,000 injured, giving a ratio of 1,700 acutely injured persons to each functioning physician. Less than 10,000 of the 65,000 hospital beds in Massachusetts would remain to accommodate more than 2,000,000 injured short-term survivors.

In a document by the Pontifical Academy of Sciences (Vatican) it is pointed out how medical assistance would be impossible because of the interruption of communications, lack of food and water, the impossibility of giving aid to the victims without exposing oneself to lethal radiation, the general social breakdown, infections, irreversible brain damage to the unborn, heavy increase in cancer and genetic damage for coming generations, if any. "Prevention is our only way out". (From "Carece de realidad médica afirmar que se puede sobrevivir a una guerra nuclear", *Información,* Alicante, 24 December 1981)

16 ". . . global fallout from a total explosive yield of 10,000 Mt . . . would cause in the order of 5 to 10 million additional deaths from cancer within the next 40 years. In addition, a similar amount of (non-lethal) thyroid cancers would result. Genetic damage would appear in as many instances as lethal cancers, half of which would be manifest in the following two generations and the rest in generations thereafter" (45, p. 79).

"Thirty years after the attack the population of the UK will have declined – from all causes – to about 10 millions" (5, p. 240).

The UNEP report states (49, p. 38) "The hazards of war do not end with the coming of peace. Unexploded mines, bombs and shells can hamper mineral exploitation, make land unsafe to farm, hamper development and endanger people who disturb them". "One government reported that it had cleared 14,469,600 land mines, and that clearance was continuing at the rate of 300,000 to 400,000 a year. . . . The country most seriously affected reported that the remnants of war had killed 3,834 people, most of them children . . .".

17 For a discussion of the relation between catastrophe and suicide, see Leugering (30). He does not discuss nuclear catastrophe or cataclysm, however. Suicide, like euthanasia, will probably be a widespread phenomenon under such conditions of hopelessness.

18 "At Hiroshima and Nagasaki there *were* severe social effects even though outside help was received and the crisis relatively brief: those who survived became the 'Hibakusha' (meaning 'survivors') who could no longer relate to normal existence – *they suffered guilt at having survived* and for all those directly inolved there was loss of psychological 'anchoring points' – the physical environment and customary lifestyles" (5, p. 224).

19 "The methods are weakest, given the imponderables, in the calculation of longer-term and indirect effects; the additional tens of millions of deaths in the days and weeks immediately after a nuclear attack, the further millions (or tens of millions) of attack-related deaths in the ensuing months or years, the calculation of deaths resulting from the unavailability of medical care or other social support systems, and the long-term economic and social damage resulting from disruption and disorganization of the social fabric rather than from direct and immediate destruction" (15a, p. 959).

According to the UN study (45, p. 82). "The major cause of hunger today is poverty – the lack of resources with which to buy enough food or enough fertilizers, fuels, machinery, etc., for an adequate indigenous production. This would be even more pronounced after a large nuclear war". Unfortunately, the study fails to indicate what is the source of that poverty. That "all countries would suffer a drastic reduction of foreign trade, entailing difficulties and economic losses" goes without saying, but the study is too uncritical about foreign trade and financial transactions, not pointing out the negative aspects, such as lack of mobilization of own resources, dependency, even exploitation. A more realistic approach would see a nuclear war not as an end to all trade; "A failure to achieve viability (i.e. production at least equalling consumption plus depreciation) would result in many additional deaths and much additional economic, political and social deterioration" (45, p. 84). It would also look into the restructuring of trade, the obvious predominance of South–South trade if the North is greatly destroyed and the need to mobilize own resources better.

20 This presupposes that nuclear powers have not eliminated such competitors in advance by sending bombs in their direction.

CHAPTER 4.

1 As the UN study puts it (45, p. 95): "In the nuclear age, however, the very cornerstone of what is projected as defence is offensive capability, while defensive capabilities in the true sense of that word – are very limited". The UN study does nothing to improve this situation, however.

2 "ABM defence capabilities are limited by the Treaty concluded under the terms of the first SALT agreement of 1972 and of the Protocol to that Treaty signed in Moscow in 1974. The ABM Treaty indicated that both super-Powers were prepared to continue to rely on the concept of deterrence as a basic feature of their strategic relationship. Concluding this Treaty, they both implicitly acknowledged that their respective high value targets must remain hostage in case of aggression by the other" (45, p. 96).

3 Desmond Ball, in a study prepared for the International Institute for Strategic Studies in London, concludes that "there can really be no possibility of controlling nuclear war . . . nuclear weapons are simply too powerful and have too many [unpredictable] effects to be used in a precise and discriminatory fashion". Leaders on both sides will lose the ability to control any escalation of hostilities as their command facilities are knocked out of action and leaders come under political pressure to act. Thus, limited nuclear strikes are unrealistic as a part of the Western overall concept of deterrence, because command facilities are too vulnerable and because it is doubtful whether the Soviet Union will cooperate in any US attempt to limit nuclear exchanges (from report on the study in *International Herald Tribune,* 29 October 1981, p. 2).

4 For precise details about the US location of likely major destruction in a nuclear war, see the Atlas prepared for this purpose (56, pp. 10–11). There are some concentrated risk areas, such as the Washington-New York-Boston megalopolitan area: but otherwise relatively dispersed, with the Rocky Mountains and the prairie states showing a lower concentration of high risk areas.

5 The UN study has the following view of the matter (45, p. 87): "Civil defence is sometimes regarded between the Super-Powers as a component of the strategic balance and it is then even maintained that a strong civil defence effort could upset the balance. This seems to be an exaggeration of

current civil defence capabilities, as in our time no civil defence system could provide reliable protection for most of the citizenry under all circumstances". The latter is of course true, but misses the point. First, civil defense could be substantially improved. Secondly even if it is not, evacuating and sheltering large parts of the population would (1) signal to the other side that "we are ready", for your first strike or for your second strike as a response to our first strike, and (2) signal to military commanders on both sides that the field is now ready for action; one does not have to consider major civilian casualties. Both factors could greatly contribute to the tension. Needless to say, for a country with no offensive capability these mechanisms do not work: civil defense would simply be one more dimension of invulnerability.

6 As an example of how offensive weapons systems and dependency on overextended eco-cycles are related the famous argument by the then US Secretary of Defense, Harold Brown, can be quoted:
"In 1978, our imports of goods and services amounted to $229 billion. Exports were $225 billion, or around 10 percent of our Gross National Product. Our direct foreign investments amounted to $168 billion. With time and a reduction in our standard of living, we could forego or substitute for much of what we import. But any major interruption of this flow of goods and services could have the most serious nearterm effects on the U.S. economy. In no respect is this more evident than in the case of oil. A large-scale disruption in the supply of foreign oil could have as damaging consequences for the United States as the loss of an important military campaign, or indeed a war". (From Brown, H. Annual Report for Fiscal Year 1981. US Department of Defense, Washington DC, 1980; quoted here from 11, p. 55)

This factor is seen by another US politician (Interior Secretary James G. Watt), who talks about the US dependence on the Soviet Union and South Africa for strategic resources, "America is dependent for the majority of strategic materials needed for military might on [these] two foreign sources" (*IHT*, 14 January 1982). And here is the wartime aspect of the same:
"Overseas supplies will be abruptly cut off by the destruction of ports, whilst shipments at sea will turn around, their crews and owners neither wishing to become involved in nuclear war nor to deliver . . . where payment is most unlikely. Fresh produce will be at a premium, probably throughout the whole northern hemisphere" (5, p. 226).

7 The UN study itself points to alternative, defensive defense (45, p. 47): "There are indications that the introduction of highly efficient, precision-guided conventional missiles or other munitions (smart weapons) might render the tactical nuclear option less attractive to military commanders in the future". This is not developed into a more coherent alternative, however.

8 " . . . power is also power to fight on somebody else's territory, meaning that Center powers will try to have fighting on Periphery territory or Marginal territory if they can manage to do so". (15, p. 5). Needless to say, this is the kind of factor that increases the destructiveness of war very much – not only is the fighting far away from home, but it is even away from the key adversary. "What it [the Center system, the key belligerents of the Second World War in Europe] exported to the Arab soil of what today is the Libyan Arab Jamahiriya was more than its Center-Center war: it was also the testing of massive tank battles under ideal conditions (except for the supplies)" (15, p. 8).

9 In the first line would come countries like Switzerland, Albania, Yugoslavia,

then Finland, Austria, then Sweden and France, Rumania. This is explored in some detail in Galtung, J., *Four Roads to Peace* (forthcoming, 1983).

10 As Lumsden says (32, p. 55): "It is time to see the global ecology as one, and war – and preparations for war – as totally maladaptive".

11 The Thorsson report arrives at a similar conclusion (51, p. 163): " . . . the Group has placed the disarmament–development relationship in the context of a triangular interaction between disarmament, development and security . . . the Group has argued that the arms race itself has developed into a threat to the security of nations . . .". To this there can be no objection. But then it continues " . . . and that general and complete disarmament under effective international control, particularly nuclear disarmament, would directly enhance security". One can certainly agree with the part about nuclear disarmament, but as an analysis of security this leaves out completely the striving of countries for some measure of defense in case of an attack in a world where collective defense seems insufficient, at least at present.

12 The United Nations General Assembly resolution 36/7 on the "Historical Responsibility of States for the Preservation of Nature for the Present and Future Generations" was adopted on 27 October 1981 by a recorded vote of 80 in favor to none against with 55 abstentions (the year before, 30 October 1980, the vote was 68–0–47). The resolution requests the Secretary General, with the cooperation of UNEP and on the basis of the studies in progress and the views of States, to complete a report with recommendations for the acceptance by States "of specific measures relating to the protection of nature from the pernicious effects of the arms race, and to the limitation and prohibition of types of military activity which present the greatest danger to nature". The resolution was sponsored by the Eastern European group and introduced by the Soviet Union. Western European countries and the USA felt UNEP was not the forum.

13 Kovda gives as an example (27, p. 52) the enormous amount needed to halt desertification in the world, according to the UN World Desertification Control Conference in 1977: "They total to $30 thousand million by the year 2000. This is no small sum of money. But it exceeds the size of the expenditure on the arms and the war preparations only by a sum which is spent on the latter during 15 days".

CHAPTER 5.

1 A picture of the UN view of the desirable state of affairs is given in Article 111 in the Final Document from the First Special Session of the General Assembly on Disarmament, 1978: "General and complete disarmament under strict and effective international control shall permit States to have at their disposal only those non-nuclear forces, armaments, facilities and establishments that are agreed to be necessary to maintain internal order and protect the personal security of citizens in order that States shall support and provide agreed manpower for a United Nations peace force". This is a model of an alternative security system, but at best, it seems, a long-term model.

2 Today it is touching to read the early documents on conversion, from the early sixties:
"The Group is unanimously of the opinion that all the problems and difficulties of transition connected with disarmament could be met by appropriate national and international measures. There should thus be no doubt that the diversion to peaceful purposes of the resources now in military use

could be accomplished to the benefit of all countries and lead to the improvement of world economic and social conditions. The achievement of general and complete disarmament would be an unqualified blessing to all mankind", (46, p. 52, Conclusion).

"Such long-range and ambitious R&D programs might not only provide challenging work opportunities for a part of the managerial, engineering, and scientific resources now employed on defense projects but would procide constructive outlets for international rivalries, which would certainly not disappear with the advent of disarmament and would also maintain a healthy pressure on our educational system to turn out the increased flow of first-rate scientists and engineers upon which our ultimate success in this competition will likely depend". (53, p. 22, Conclusion).

Sixteen years later the concluding paragraph of the corresponding UN report was less world-centered and more United Nations-centered: "There is also a need for expert advice and assistance on a more continuous basis to follow developments closely, to advise the General Assembly, the Secretary-General and Member States on questions of disarmament, and to assist in the elaboration, specification and adjustment of targets and programmes. Improvement of the machinery of the United Nations in this direction appears to be necessary if the world Organization is to fulfill its task in the field of disarmament". (47, p. 77).

3 The Thorsson Report, (51), destined to become a classic on the interrelation between the development and military systems, discusses a very high number of conversion possibilities and problems. However, the report still fails to convince the present author on two rather major points:

(1) that *security* is obtained by a *dis*armament process that would deprive the military sector of raw materials, energy, capital, labor and research capacity. I would think much of this might still be needed for alternative national security systems, in other words in a *trans*armament process. Hence, the argument should be in terms of what could be saved in a process toward, for instance, defensive arms, not a (totally unrealistic) process towards practically speaking no arms at all.

(2) that *development* is obtained through a massive injection of raw materials, energy, capital, labor and research capacity liberated through disarmament. Development has something to do with satisfying human needs and making countries autonomous, and this depends on structures and socio-political processes more than on mere inputs into already existing production processes. Highly capital- and research-intensive production might reinforce existing patterns of maldevelopment, and autonomy will hardly be served since most of the assets released would come from superpowers and big powers who will see to it that strings are attached. On a smaller scale, and as catastrophe aid, there could be no objection of this kind, however. And that there is a negative link between disarmament and development, would seem indisputable (47, p. 73): "Development at an acceptable rate would be hard if not impossible to reconcile with a continuation of the arms race".

4 Thus, of the 1,233 known and presumed nuclear explosions between 16 July 1945 and 31 December 1979, a total of 414 months or an average of 3 (2.978) per month, 498 were in the 217 months prior to the limited test ban treaty of August 1963 or an average of 2.29 per month and 735 were in the 197 months after the treaty, or an average of 3.73 per month, in other words appreciably higher (45, p. 85). "In recent years, an average of 30 to

40 tests have been carried out annually" (45, p. 84). It is reasonable to assume that the tests underground have been important in "perfecting" the weapons we are now concerned with. Thus, the PTBT is at best an environmental treaty and not a disarmament treaty; at worst not even that. For the technical goals served by testing, see (45, p. 33), particularly "improvement of yield-to-weight ratios".

5 The support for the old idea of no-first-use for nuclear weapons given by Bundy et al. (3) implies "that any such policy would require a strengthened confidence in the adequacy of the conventional forces of the Alliance . . .". It should be noted that no-first-use is not the same as abolition, and that the distinction between nuclear and conventional is not the same as the distinction between offensive and defensive.

6 "A total nuclear war is the highest level of human madness" (45, p. 71). In a sense true, but not a very useful statement. The roots of madness do not disappear when the plant is named. It is the view of the present author, not a very original one, that the nuclear arsenal is a completely logical consequence, step by step, of conventional security doctrine, and that future military nuclear action is an equally logical consequence of present and past military preparation. In the context of such a doctrine, preparation for nuclear war, even nuclear war itself, does not appear as madness but as cool logic, pursued by cool, if somewhat narrow, minds. Hence the *doctrine* is madness because of its consequences; a strong argument, in my view, for concentrating the struggle against nuclear war on the search for alternative security doctrines.

7 That apocalyptic visions of the impact of nuclear war, however realistic they may be, do not necessarily lead to useful proposals is well illustrated in the book by Jonathan Schell (42, pp. 225–231). "I would suggest that the ultimate requirements are in essence the two that I have mentioned: global disarmament, both nuclear and conventional, and the invention of political means by which the world can peacefully settle the issues that throughout history it has settled by war". "The goal would be a nonviolent world". "Two paths lie before us. One leads to death, the other to life". Such phrases are far removed from the real world – which is not an argument against the author, it may not be his interest or his field to come closer to the real world in his laudable search for alternatives. But my point is that an inability to come up with proposals is found not only among the proponents of the nuclear race, but also among the antagonists. We are all the victims of a certain paralysis of the mind.

APPENDIX

1 I am grateful to Michael Hopkins of the ILO for drawing my attention to another use of the same approach, in *The Mapping of Interrelationships between Population and Development,* Department of International Economic and Social Affairs, United Nations, New York, 1981 (also see the more extensive *The Work of the Task Force on Inter-Relationships between Population and Development.* ESA/P/ WP. 76, November 1981). The work of this task force has some of the same strengths and weaknesses as the present approach: "for instance, inter-action effects between variables, other than those deriving from recursive relationships implicit in the matrix, are not taken into account" (*ibid* ., p. 47). Put differently: they may be taken into account, but not as a consequence of using a matrix approach.

2 "Synergism means that the response of any given organism (or material object) to two or more different stresses

applied simultaneously can be expected to exceed the simple sum of the responses to each of these stresses by itself . . . At the integrated or systems level, the interaction of components necessary for the functioning of the system will be impeded to a larger extent than the removal of certain components per se indicate". (29, p. 136).

3 Without necessarily agreeing with the example chosen it has been pointed out that the invasion of the Mongolian Tartars in the 13th to the 15th centuries interrupted the development of Russian culture for 200 to 300 years. The problem is, of course, that we do not have any consensus about what constitutes higher and lower cultures, and hence of what constitutes cultural development. But there can be no doubt that war, destruction and occupation disrupt what could be called the normal course of a culture (31, p. 213).

Selected literature
on the effects of military activity

1 Aranow, S. et al., *The Fallen Sky: Medical Consequences of Thermonuclear War,* Hill and Wang, New York, 1963.
2 Barnaby, F. and Rotblat, J., "The Effect of Nuclear Weapons", AMBIO, 1982, No. 2–3
3 Bundy, M., Kennan, G. F., NcNamara, R. S. and Smith, G., "Nuclear Weapons and the Atlantic Alliance", *Foreign Affairs,* 1982, pp. 753–768.
4 Carter, L. J., "Navy Considers Scuttling Old Nuclear Subs", *Science,* 209, pp. 1495–1497.
5 Clarke, Magnus, *The Nuclear Destruction of Britain,* Croom Helm, London.
6 Committee for the Compilation of Materials on Damage Caused by the Atomic Bombs in Hiroshima and Nagasaki, *Hiroshima and Nagasaki. The Physical, Medical, and Social Effects of the Atomic Bombings.* Basic Books, New York, 1981.
7 Congressional Research Service, Library of Congress, "The United States and Soviet Progress in Space: Summary Data through 1980 and a Forward Look", Washington, 1981.
8 Congress of the United States, *Office of Technology Assessment: The Effects of Nuclear War,* Croom Helm, London, 1980.
9 Dragsdahl, Jørgen, "Traenede Dræbere overlever dommedag", *Information,* 12–13 September 1981.
10 Dupas, Alain, "Les programmes spatiaux militaires", *La recherche,* No. 130, February 1982, pp. 259–269
11 Environmental Advisory Council, *War and Environment,* Liber, Stockholm, 1981.
12 Feld, B., "Can We Survive a Nuclear War with the Soviet Union", *Bulletin of the Atomic Scientists,* September 1979, p. 38.
13 Frank, J., *Sanity and Survival,* Cresset, London, 1967.
14 Friends Committee for National Legislation, *Newsletter,* Washington, D. C., July 1979.
15 Galtung J., "Material War Remnants: Some Sociological Observations", Paper prepared for the Symposium on Material Remnants of the Second World War on Libyan Soil, 28 April to 1 May 1981, Geneva.
15 a Geiger, H. J., "Addressing Apocalypse Now: The Effects of Nuclear Warfare as a Public Health Concern", *American Jounal of Public Health,* September 1980, pp. 958–961.
16 Glasstone, S. and Dolan, P. J., *The Effects of Nuclear Weapons.* US Dept of Defense and US Dept of Energy. Castle House Publications, London, 1980.
17 Gray, P., ed., *The Encyclopedia of the Biological Sciences,* 2nd ed, van Nostrand, New York, 1970.
18 Huisken, R., "Consumption of Raw Materials for Military Purposes", *Ambio,* 1975, No. 6, pp. 229–233.
19 Hveem, H. and Malnes, R., *Military Use of Natural Resources,* International Peace Research Institute, Oslo, 1980.
20 Höivik, Tord, "Hva skjer om SS–20 raketter settes inn mot norske militære mål?", *Ikke-vold,* Oct/Nov. 1981, pp. 4ff.
21 Ikle, F. C., *The Social Impact of Bomb Destruction* The University of Oklahoma Press, Oklahoma, 1958.
22 Iversen, Jens-Gustav, "Skader ved atomkrig i Norge", in Christoffersen

and Prydz, eds., *Atomkrig i medisinsk perspektiv.* Universitetsforlaget, Oslo, 1981, pp. 51–63.

23 deKadt, E. J., *British Defence Policy and Nuclear War,* Cass, London, 1964

24 Dessler, D. J., "Sky Reporter, Junk in Space" *Natural History,* 1982, No. 3, pp. 12–18.

25 Khozin, G., *Biosphère et Politique,* Éditions du Progrès, Moscow, 1979.

26 Kimball, C. A., "An American City Sees Absurdity", *International Herald Tribune,* 21 September 1981.

27 Kovda, V. A., "To Preserve the Biosphere – To Avert Wars" (43).

28 Krieger, D., *Disarmament and Development,* The Challenge of the International Control and Management of Dual–Purpose Technologies, Foundation for Reshaping the International Order, Rotterdam, 1981.

29 Larsson, T. "The Environmental Effects of Nuclear War", in (11).

30 Leugering, N., "Katastrophen, Unfälle, Suizide und Sozialstruktur: Konvergenzen zweier Forschningsbereiche", SIFKU-Informationen, 1981, No. 2, pp. 23–36.

31 Lohns, K. and Westing, A. H., "Umweltkrig oder Abrüstung", *Wissenschaft und Fortschritt,* 1982, No. 32, pp. 64–68.

32 Lumsden, M., "The Use of Raw Materials, Land and Water for Armament and War", in (11).

33 Martin, Brian, "How the Peace Movement Should Be Preparing for Nuclear War", *Bulletin of Peace Proposals,* 1982 No. 2.

34 Melman, S., "On the Social Costs of U.S. Militarism", *American Journal of Public Health,* 1980, No. 9, pp. 953–63.

35 Nagai, T., *We of Nagasaki,* Meredith Press, New York, 1969.

36 Nazarov, I. M., "Nuclear Tests: Man and the Environment", (43, pp. 38–41).

37 Neel, J. V., "Genetic Effects of Atomic Bombs", *Science,* 1981, No 4513 (Editorial).

38 Novikov, R., *Environment and Development,* Report by the Government of the USSR, United Nations, Economic Commission for Europe, ENV/Sem.11/R. 12, 1979.

39 Novikov, R. A., "Environmental Protection and Arms Race: Irreconcilable Contradiction" (in 43, pp. 15–19).

40 Physicians for Social Responsibility, "The Medical Consequences of Thermonuclear War", *The New England Journal of Medicine,* 1962, pp. 1126–1155.

41 Robinson, J. P., *The Effects of Weapons on Ecosystems,* Pergamon Press, Oxford, 1979 (for UNEP)

41 a Rotblat, J., *Nuclear Radiation in Warfare,* Taylor & Francis, London, 1981 (for SIPRI).

42 Schell, J., *The Fate of the Earth,* Knopf, New York, 1982.

43 Scientific Research Council on Peace and Disarmament, *Disarmament and Environment,* Nauka, Moscow, 1981.

44 United Nations Centre for Disarmament, *Economic and Social Consequences of Disarmament and of Military Expenditures,* United Nations, New York, 1978.

45 United Nations Centre for Disarmament, *Comprehensive Study on Nuclear Weapons,* United Nations, New York, 1981 (A/35/392).

46 United Nations Department of Economic and Social Affairs, *Economic and Social Consequences of Disarmament,* New York, 1962.

47 United Nations Department of Political and Security Council Affairs, *Economic and Social Consequences of the Arms Race and of Military Expenditures,* United Nations, New York, 1978.

48 United Nations, Department of Public Information, *Disarmament Fact Sheets,* No. 9, New York, October 1979.

49 United Nations Environment Programme, "The Environmental Effects of Military Activity", in *The State of the Environment 1980* Nairobi, 1981.

50 United Nations General Assembly, Special Session on Disarmament *Final Document,* New York 1978.

51 United Nations General Assembly, *Study on the Relationship between Disarmament and Development,* A/36/356, New York, 1981.

52 United Nations General Assembly, *Marine Pollution,* (A/36/452;1981)

53 United States Arms Control and Disarmament Agency. *Economic Impacts of Disarmament,* Washington, 1962.

54 United States Congress, Joint Committee on Atomic Energy, *Biological and Environmental Effects of Nuclear War: Summary Analysis of Hearings. June 22–26, 1959,* Washington, 1959.

55 United States Department of Defense, *In Combat, In Community, Saving Lives Together,* Washington, no date.

56 United States Federal Emergence Management Agency, *High Risk Areas, For Civil Nuclear Defense Planning Purposes.* TR-82, Washington, September 1979.

57 Westin, G., *Gult regn,* Dagbladet, Oslo, 30 December 1981.

58 Westing, A.H., *Weapons of Mass Destruction and the Environment* Taylor & Francis, London, 1977 (for SIPRI).

59 Westing, A.H., "Neutron Bombs and the Environment", AMBIO, 1978, pp. 93–97.

60 Westing, A.H., *Warfare in a Fragile World,* Taylor & Francis, London, 1980 (for SIPRI).

61 Westing, A.H., "Military Preparations and the Environment", in Czechoslovak Peace Committee, *Peace, Energy and the Environment,* Prague, 1981, pp. 55–65.

62 Westing, A. H., "Environmental Impact of Nuclear Warfare" *Environmental Conservation,* 1981, pp. 269–273.

63 Wetzel, K. G., "Effects on Freshwater System", AMBIO, 1982, No. 2–3.

64 World Bank *World Development Report 1979,* Washington, 1979.